FIRE
IN THE
PULPIT

by Dr. John N. Hamblin

SWORD of the LORD PUBLISHERS

Post Office Box 1099 • Murfreesboro, Tennessee 37133

Printed and Bound in the United States of America

FIRE
IN THE
PULPIT

To

My dear wife, Mrs. Cari Lynn Hamblin. For well over two decades she has wonderfully kept the "home fires" burning while I have traveled across America preaching the Word of God. If I had 'the tongue of men and angels,' I still could not articulate my appreciation for her support, sacrifice and supplication. Thank you for being my biggest cheerleader!

Contents

Foreword

In great conferences all across North America I've been delighted to share the platform and preach alongside Dr. John Hamblin. I've heard him preach most of the material in *Fire in the Pulpit*. Believe me, when he mounts the pulpit, the fire is already lit in his heart, and in short order the fire materializes in his preaching.

For over twenty years Dr. Hamblin has been busily engaged as an evangelist. In a day when compromise is rampant, here is a man who has stood tall and true in churches large and small throughout the land. In a religious environment that has made teaching the norm, this man is a preacher cut from the cloth of a Biblical prophet. He preaches somewhere in the world almost every day of his life. Whether before two dozen or two thousand, he is always upbeat, always excited and always operating full throttle.

The fickle, the fainty and the flighty will no doubt be troubled by what they read here. Admittedly, it is not the watered-down soup that is standard fare in most religious publishing. It is for that very reason that we commend it to you as something we believe you should read.

It has been my privilege to know Dr. Hamblin for a good number of years. What I have discovered has been refreshing.

FOREWORD

Personally he is a kind, polite and gentle man.

Spiritually he is a man of prayer, moral integrity and unimpeachable character.

Ministerially, he is faithful, fruitful and fervent.

Doctrinally he is theologically straight, hermeneutically solid and scripturally sound.

Evangelistically he is a testimony, a witness and a soul-winner.

Ecclesiastically he is discerning, principled and separated.

Philosophically he is "stedfast, unmoveable, always abounding in the work of the Lord" (I Cor. 15:58).

Therefore it is my delight to recommend both the man and his message. I believe that your perusal of these pages will be edifying, encouraging and a blessing.

DR. SHELTON SMITH

Chapter 1

FIRE! FIRE! FIRE!

"Then took they him, and led him, and brought him into the high priest's house. And Peter followed afar off.

"And when they had kindled a fire in the midst of the hall, and were set down together, Peter sat down among them.

"But a certain maid beheld him as he sat by the fire, and earnestly looked upon him, and said, This man was also with him.

"And he denied him, saying, Woman, I know him not.

"And after a little while another saw him, and said, Thou art also of them. And Peter said, Man, I am not.

"And about the space of one hour after another confidently affirmed, saying, Of a truth this fellow also was with him: for he is a Galilæan.

"And Peter said, Man, I know not what thou sayest. And immediately, while he yet spake, the cock crew.

"And the Lord turned, and looked upon Peter. And Peter remembered the word of the Lord, how he had said unto him, Before the cock crow, thou shalt deny me thrice.

"And Peter went out, and wept bitterly."—Luke 22:54–62.

During the spiritual life of every believer, there will be times when he or she will be found before the glowing embers of some spiritual flame. This is true of the newest

1

convert to the oldest member. While some of these blazes would be considered minuses, others would have to be classified as pluses.

There were three instances where Peter was drawn to a fire. And like him, we also are drawn to the same three distinct flames.

I. THE FIRE OF REPROACH

The believer can be drawn to the fire of reproach.

"But a certain maid beheld him as he sat by the fire, and earnestly looked upon him, and said, This man was also with him.

"And he denied him, saying, Woman, I know him not."— vss. 56, 57.

Peter followed the Lord Jesus Christ from a distance; at a large fire in the high priest's courtyard, he denied his Master.

The fervent lips that had once said, "I am ready to go with thee, both into prison, and to death" (vs. 33), now became the failing lips that said, "I know him not."

The songwriter Robert Robinson must have known something about this narrative and his own nature, for he picked up his pen and wrote these stirring words:

> **Prone to wander, Lord, I feel it;**
> **Prone to leave the God I love.**
> **Here's my heart, oh, take and seal it;**
> **Seal it for Thy courts above.**

We can be drawn to the fire of reproach.

Philippians 2:15 says, "That ye may be blameless and harmless, the sons of God, without rebuke, in the midst of a crooked and perverse nation, among whom ye shine as world."

When the believer gets to the sad place where he is standing with the world and saying, either by word or deed, "I know not Jesus," he has significantly diminished the light of his personal testimony.

The closer a Christian gets to the Lord, the more intense the light of his personal testimony shines. But the farther he gets from the Lord and the closer he gets to the world, the dimmer his personal testimony gets. It is impossible for a Christian to line up with the world and have a bright, clear personal testimony for Jesus.

Every Christian has a testimony—it's either a good, bright testimony or a bad, dim testimony. How close you are to the Lord and how far away you are from the world determines the degree of brightness.

Several years ago I held a revival in Michigan, and one night on the way home I stopped at a service station to get gasoline. When I paid the attendant, I also gave him a gospel tract. He looked at it and without the slightest hesitation said, "I'm saved."

I was startled somewhat, because he had long, greasy hair and a wild, unkempt beard and an earring in one earlobe. I didn't check to see if he had pumps and a purse to go with his outfit, but I did question him about his conversion, and he gave a testimony that rang true.

Then he said, "Not only am I saved, but I was also going to a fundamental Bible college because God had called me to preach. Then I broke a rule, and they kicked me out."

I asked, "Which school were you attending?"

He said, "I'm sure you've never heard of it. It's a Bible

college called the Midwestern Baptist College in Pontiac, Michigan."

As I walked away, I thought, *Instead of taking receipts for gasoline, he ought to be somewhere preaching the Gospel.*

What happened to him? He went too close to the world and ended up next to the fire of reproach.

II. THE FIRE OF RESTORATION

The believer can also be drawn to the fire of restoration.

"As soon then as they were come to land, they saw a fire of coals there, and fish laid thereon, and bread."—John 21:9.

When the apostle Peter learned that Jesus was on the shore, he put on his coat, jumped into the water and was the first to set foot on the beach.

Peter found the resurrected Christ standing before a warm fire with a delicious meal already prepared.

Now, dear Christians, do not miss the wonderful truth here. The fire represents family and forgiveness. The coals represent compassion and cleansing. The fish represent forbearance and fellowship. The bread represents benevolence and blessing.

I am glad that God doesn't give up on His children. No matter how cold our hearts, how far we are from Him or how complacent we become, we can still be drawn to the fire of restoration. And He never disowns any of His children. God is interested in seeing that all of us who are not right with Him, get right with Him.

Don't ever get into the mind-set or put it into your head that once a saved person messes up his life or gets away from the Lord that God can never use him again. Don't ever even entertain that thought, because it is not between the covers of the Bible.

When we look at Peter's life, we discover there are several things that wayward believers can do after they've come back to God.

1. They can run. "Then arose Peter, and ran unto the sepulchre" (Luke 24:12).

Just because a Christian stumbles does not mean that he is to throw away his spiritual track shoes—he can run!

2. They can become a reliable witness. "The Lord is risen indeed, and hath appeared to Simon" (vs. 34).

God's Word still carries immeasurable weight, even if the one who handles it once had an imperfect walk.

3. They can rejoice. "They worshipped him, and returned to Jerusalem with great joy" (vs. 52).

If no Christians but those who never backslid could shout it out, then our churches would be as silent as a cemetery.

Oh, that every single believer would realize the outstanding things that the wayward believer can do after he comes back to God!

I read about a friend who showed a costly handkerchief to John Ruskin, a well-known artist. On it was an ink stain.

"Nothing can be done with it now," said the owner. "It is absolutely worthless."

Mr. Ruskin made no reply but carried it away with him. After a time he sent it back to his friend, who could scarcely believe his eyes. In a most skillful and creative way, the artist had used Indian ink to make the stain the center for a design.

Christian, aren't you glad that a blotted life is not a ruined life if it but goes to the Artist of restoration?

III. THE FIRE OF REVIVAL

Not only can the believer be drawn to the fire of reproach and the fire of restoration, but he can also be drawn to the fire of revival.

"There appeared unto them cloven tongues like as of fire, and it sat upon each of them."—Acts 2:3.

The apostle Peter was in the Upper Room on the day of Pentecost when the power of God filled not only that chamber but also those Christians.

Don't miss it now: the symbol God selected to signify supernatural power was fire resting upon the saints.

D. L. Moody, the great and mightily used evangelist of bygone years, once said, "I do not know of anything America needs more today than men and women on fire with the fire of Heaven."

Friends, we can be drawn to the fire of revival.

Matthew 3:11 says, "He shall baptize you with the Holy Ghost, and with fire."

When the people of God convene in some great meeting, it is not just about good singing, although we hear great singing. It's not just about the preachers' messages or the saints of God's fellowshipping one with another. The purpose, the plan and the projected goal of such a meeting is revival in each life. That will come when we are drawn to the fire of revival.

Whenever any believer is touched by the flame of a spiritual awakening, he is always quick to speak to someone about his soul. That's how you can tell whether or not you're having revival.

Some folks think that they're having revival because they have sent out fliers to surrounding churches and gone through the neighborhoods passing out handbills (with the evangelist's high school graduation picture on it). I'm all for that, but no amount of fliers and handbills will bring revival.

Some think revival comes with the evangelist. I'm certainly not throwing stones at the Bible office of the evangelist, but he doesn't bring revival with him.

A lady once said to me, "What is an evangelist?" She had not been saved very long, and I was the first evangelist she'd ever met.

I said, "An evangelist is a spiritual alarm clock."

She said, "I thought an evangelist was a preacher who blew in, blew up and then blew out!"

I said, "Well, yes, we're that too."

I don't think I've ever heard anyone say, "Oh, how I love to hear my alarm clock ringing in the morning! It's the sweetest thing I've ever heard, and I could just listen to it for a long time." But if you want revival, then you must rise and shine, accept and heed the human alarm clock's message.

Revival is not just about the evangelist; it's not just about five consecutive days of special services; revival happens when folks are interested again in the destiny of people's souls and in endeavoring to reach them with the Gospel.

Some time ago I was on my way to a meeting, and before I got to the church, I passed a little restaurant that showed signs of devastation and destruction. On the marquee above the restaurant were these words: "Out of Business Because of Fire."

I thought, *The Christian is **in** business to win people to the Lord, to get out the Gospel, to tell about Jesus—**because of the fire**.*

Gipsy Smith was in a meeting one night, and when he walked into the inquiry room, he found there a little boy who had come forward to be saved. Gipsy Smith personally knelt with this lad and led him to the Lord Jesus Christ.

The little boy said, "What do I do now that I'm saved?"

He said, "You leave yourself with Jesus, and you go on to serve Him and to win others to Him."

The little boy smiled and left. The next night during the invitation the same little boy was back in the inquiry room. Gipsy Smith said, "I thought you got saved last night."

The little boy's eyes sparkled like stars. "I did, but I came tonight to bring my mother to Jesus."

There's more. The next night the little boy was again in the inquiry room, this time with his grandfather.

Here was a young child who, because of being at the fire of revival, brought two generations in his own family to the Lord Jesus Christ.

It doesn't matter how long you've been saved; when you get to the fire of revival, you'll go after those who are lost.

Peter stood before a fire at three different times, at three different places.

Every Christian is standing before either the fire of reproach, the fire of restoration or the fire of revival. Dear Christian friend, before which fire are you standing now?

Chapter 2

LEAVE THE ANCIENT LANDMARKS ALONE!

"Remove not the ancient landmark, which thy fathers have set."—Prov. 22:28.

Today we find ourselves living in a time when Bible landmarks are being forcibly changed. What was once an absolute is now called an antique. Consequently, many good Christians are losing their direction all because of the displacing of landmarks.

As we can see in the text verse, God has given clear command regarding the old property markers: "Remove not." The word *remove* means *to change place in any manner.*

Eastern fields were not divided by hedges or walls or ditches. In order to avoid the confusion, natural property lines were established: riverbeds, tributary streams and edges of valleys. But in the open ground, the separate properties were marked by a deep furrow or a large stone almost buried in the soil.

So important was the location of a landmark that a woeful curse was pronounced upon those who would tamper with it. The Bible says, "Cursed be he that removeth his neighbour's landmark" (Deut. 27:17).

9

Instead of trying to be "contemporary" by removing the ancient landmarks, we need to return to many of them.

Christians must decide that they are not going to move the old spiritual property markers which identify the eternal verities of our faith.

Just a few days ago a missionary said to me, "I fear that many good churches are only one pastor away from modernism." We need to decide with unbending determination that we are going to leave the landmarks where God has in His wisdom so deliberately and so definitively placed them.

At the very foundations of the Christian faith there are at least three ancient property markers that must not be moved. They are so important, so essential to all that is important to us, that we must leave them alone.

I. THE PERFECT SCRIPTURES

"All scripture is given by inspiration of God, and is profitable for doctrine, for reproof, for correction, for instruction in righteousness:

"That the man of God may be perfect, throughly furnished unto all good works."—II Tim. 3:16, 17.

God gave to man His complete Word, His will and His way between the covers of one wonderful Book. The man of God can be correct in every detail of his ministry if he heeds the message from God's Great Book, for it is correct in every detail.

Sir Walter Scott wrote these heart-penetrating words:

> **Within this awful volume lies**
> **The mystery of mysteries.**
> **Happiest they of human race**
> **To whom their God hath given grace**

**To read, to fear, to hope, to pray,
To lift the latch, to force the way;
But better had they ne'er been born
That read to doubt or read to scorn.**

"For the prophecy came not in old time by the will of man: but holy men of God spake as they were moved by the Holy Ghost"—II Pet. 1:21.

Today fundamental Christians are being bombarded by critics who say that the Bible contains hundreds of mistakes, that the Word of God was not really written word for word, God just gave man a basic outline and let him fill in the rest, that one version is just as reliable as another.

A mechanic was called to repair the mechanism of a giant telescope. During the noon hour the chief astronomer came to the man and found him reading the Bible.

"What do you expect from that?" he asked. "The Bible is out of date, and we don't even know who wrote it."

The mechanic pondered for a moment, then looked up and said, "Don't you make a considerable use of the multiplication table in your calculations?"

"Yes, of course."

"Do you know who wrote it?"

"No, I guess I don't."

"Then how can you trust the multiplication table when you don't know who wrote it."

"We trust it because...well...because it works," the astronomer answered a bit testily.

"Well, I trust the Bible for the same reason: it works."

Christian, don't move the ancient landmark of the Bible—because it still works! You and I ought to get excited when we hear the pure, unadulterated, preserved Word of God. It is the perfect Scripture, God's own Word! Don't tamper with it!

II. THE PRECIOUS SON OF GOD

"And lo a voice from heaven, saying, This is my beloved Son, in whom I am well pleased."—Matt. 3:17.

At the baptism of the Lord Jesus Christ by John the Baptist in the river Jordan, God the Father gave His verbal approval of God the Son.

On this hallowed occasion, all three members of the Trinity were present: the Beloved Son, the Holy Spirit in the form of a dove, and the Heavenly Father speaking from Heaven.

The ancient landmark of the precious Son should be left in place.

Phillips Brooks once said, "Jesus Christ, the condescension of divinity, and the exaltation of humanity."

Today we are being told by the pseudointellectual thinkers that Jesus is not any different than other spiritual teachers, that He was just another one of the religious leaders who appeared on the pages of human history, that He was nothing more than an unsuccessful political revolutionary. Every one of those devilish statements is a subtle attempt to move an old spiritual landmark, a property marker. Each such case is an attack against the Son of God Himself. You had better leave it alone!

Jesus is not merely a religious leader followed by lost people! Jesus is not just a teacher who appeared on the pages of human history! Jesus is not a failed, unsuccessful, frustrated, political revolutionist!

The evidence is abundant to certify that Jesus is the Son of God.

1. There is the evidence of His sermons. "He taught them as one having authority, and not as the scribes" (Matt. 7:29).

Where the religious leaders put a question mark on their teaching, the Redeemer put a strong exclamation point!

2. There is the evidence of His supernatural deeds. "When the sun was setting, all they that had any sick with divers diseases brought them unto him; and he laid his hands on every one of them, and healed them" (Luke 4:40).

He healed everyone brought to Him. Every fevered brow that He cooled, every violent storm that He calmed, every vile demon that He cast out, every crooked limb that He straightened cried out, "He is God's darling Son!"

If these so-called faith healers had what they claimed to have, they'd easily empty out the hospitals, funeral homes and cemeteries. The naive and gullible cry out, saying, "But how do you explain their miracles?"

I explain them in one of two ways: one, trickery; two, demonic power. The Bible says, "And the beast was taken, and with him the false prophet that wrought miracles before him....These both were cast alive into a lake of fire burning with brimstone" (Rev. 19:20).

The so-called faith healers do the same thing that "the false prophet" can do. They are dishonest, used-religious salesmen! Most of them are spiritual ripoff artists. And yet born-again Christians not only watch them, but they support them with donations to their "ministries"! These same Christians attend Sunday morning, Sunday night and Wednesday night services at their independent, fundamental churches; and when they hear their faithful pastor preaching the Word of God, they fold their arms, set their jaws and say, "I'll have to check out that sermon to see if he's right." Where do they go to verify the preacher's words? To the Bible? No! They go to the television preachers! Somebody sound the alarm! Wake up the folks! Nap time is over! Get real on this!

3. There is the evidence of His stone. "And they found the stone rolled away from the sepulchre" (Luke 24:2).

The investigation of the Lord Jesus Christ's identity is forever settled at the entrance of an empty tomb.

Oh, that every one of us would realize that the pieces of evidence which prove that Jesus is the Son of God are His sermons, His supernatural deeds and His stone that was "rolled away"!

Several symbols are commonly employed to represent Christianity. The cross is the most-noted symbol. In the days of religious persecution of the early church, Christians used the fish to identify one another. But "the stone" is also a symbol of Christianity.

As a missionary finished preaching in a marketplace in one of the villages of northern India, a Muslim walked up to him and said, "You must admit that we have one thing that is far better than anything that you have."

"What is that you have?"

"We can go to Mecca and find a coffin," he said. "But when you Christians go to Jerusalem, your Mecca, you find nothing but an empty grave."

The minister smiled and said, "That's just the difference. Muhammad is dead and in his coffin. Jesus is risen and alive forever more!"

All false systems of religion and philosophy are related to a coffin, but Christ is risen, and all power in Heaven and on earth is given to Him. He is alive forever more!

> **I serve a risen Saviour;**
> **He's in the world today.**
> **I know that He is living,**
> **Whatever men may say.**
> **I see His hand of mercy,**
> **I hear His voice of cheer,**
> **And just the time I need Him,**
> **He's always near.**

Leave the landmark of the precious Son alone.

> **Low in the grave He lay—**
> **Jesus my Saviour!**
> **Waiting the coming day—**
> **Jesus my Lord!**
>
> **Up from the grave He arose,**
> **With a mighty triumph o'er His foes;**
> **He arose a Victor from the dark domain,**
> **And He lives forever with His saints to reign.**
> **He arose! He arose! Hallelujah! Christ arose!**

III. THE PRIORITY OF SOUL WINNING

"And he said unto them, Go ye into all the world, and preach the gospel to every creature."—Mark 16:15.

"And that repentance and remission of sins should be preached in his name among all nations, beginning at Jerusalem."—Luke 24:47.

At His divine ascension, the Lord Jesus Christ gave to His disciples the direct assignment and the defining agenda of world evangelization.

Jesus left no doubt as to the church's number one duty and the Christian's number one objective. The official mandate of Jesus to us is to get every person on this planet to put his faith in Him as his personal Saviour.

The main thing every day is keeping people out of Hell. It is pushing hard, propagating hard and pressing hard the glorious Gospel that people might be saved. Everything else is secondary and ought to take a back seat; in fact, some things ought not to even be in the back seat.

Getting out the Gospel, whether it be by passing out gospel tracts, inviting folks to church, going soul winning door-to-door, or just telling people far and near that Jesus saves is our mission!

I didn't write this; I just recite it. I'm just a newsboy who is shouting, "Read all about it!" If you mess with the priority of soul winning, you are tampering with a landmark; and God said, in no uncertain terms, that would bring a curse upon you (Deut. 27:17).

Today we hear, "Before you give anyone the Gospel, find out what spiritual gift you have been given." I realize that different people have different gifts, but that's not our first priority.

My spiritual gift is this: I am to tell you that you are not supposed to wait until you find out what your spiritual gift

16

is before you give someone the Gospel!

"Just live a good testimony before your family, neighbors and business associates. And when they want what you have, they'll come to you." That's not in the Word of God. The Bible says that we are to proclaim His message. Those who say anything different are only trying to soothe their back-slidden consciences. If you ask them, "How many folks have witnessed your testimony and come to you and asked how to be saved?" they'll stammer and stutter and probably get upset with you because you've caught them in the trap of lifestyle evangelism.

A young man surrendered to preach, went off to a fundamental Bible college and later candidated in an independent, fundamental church. He called me afterwards and said, "There was a real dead spirit there. I taught Sunday school, I preached Sunday morning and Sunday night, and I felt like they had hung black crepe on the front door. There was a spirit of death everywhere. I told them that my emphasis was on soul winning, and that went over like a cement plow."

I said, "They used to have a visitation program, right?"

"They used to, but nobody came."

"And they used to have a bus ministry."

"Yes, but they couldn't keep a bus captain, and they didn't want to make payments on a bus that would just sit and rust."

"And the tract rack has only tracts about defending the Faith and protecting some doctrine but nothing about the plan of salvation or how to keep somebody out of Hell. Now, don't misunderstand me, we need to defend the Faith! I make it known as often as I can that it is high time that we stop playing checkers with charismatics, lawn darts with liberals, pat-a-cake with the pope and board games with modernists. I try on every possible occasion to sound the alarm. We need not only to defend the Faith, but we need to proclaim the Gospel as well!"

He said, "You're exactly right."

Every one of these double-dealing statements is a subtle attempt to move an old spiritual property marker. Leave that landmark alone!

"But," they say, "soul winning doesn't work like it used to." Then you must not be working at it, or you would know that it does. In the word *work*, let me advise you, there are prayers, perspiration and perseverance. Too many Christians just hit a lick here and dig around a little bit there and then expect God to bless their *efforts*. No! Soul winning is a work, and it is work.

I was in a meeting recently in Cambridge, Ohio. As I walked through the lobby of the hotel to go to the meeting, I stopped at the desk and gave the clerk a gospel tract. Our conversation took no longer than ten seconds.

The next night I made the same trek from my room through the lobby, and the clerk said, "Mister, I want you to know that during my break I read that thing you gave me last night, and I asked the Lord to save me. I want you to know, the next time you come to town I'm going to come hear your *mass!*" He didn't know all the vocabulary, but He was obviously on the road to victory!

It still works, and we ought to leave alone the landmark of soul winning!

Last year in one of my meetings, some people got mad at me; and in the midst of my preaching, five people literally stood up and walked out of the church. I couldn't help but see them. But I thought they had an appointment, so I didn't think anymore about it.

As I walked out of the church, those same five people were standing on the front sidewalk—guilt and sin written all over their countenances. They looked at me as if I were the Grim Reaper. I just thanked them for coming to the service and walked toward my vehicle.

The five of them chose the woman among them to be their spokesperson. Wasn't that wonderful? She came up beside me and commenced to rip me to shreds.

"We don't like the way you preach! We don't like that intensity in your delivery! We don't like bombastic preaching! We don't like it when you raise your voice. We don't like your sick sense of humor." (That last one offended me!) She kept on like a chain saw, buzzing after me with no letup.

When she finally paused for a breath, I said, "Let me ask you this? You heard me last night; you heard some of me tonight. Did I preach the Bible?"

"Oh yes, very clear."

"Then you and I have nothing further to discuss!"

As soon as I told this woman that she had nothing to talk to me about, she started in again. She followed me all over that parking lot, growling all the way. Suddenly a man in a tee shirt and shorts jumped in front of me, shook his finger in my face and said, "You're Dr. Hamblin, aren't you?"

I was trying to change gears mentally from the Hillsdale Hag who had been snapping at my heels to another member of her posse. I said, "Yes, I am," and I braced for another assault.

19

He said, "Someone left a flier in my door. It was an invitation to come hear Dr. John Hamblin preach. I couldn't believe it—my name is Bob Hamblin. I have a brother whose name was John, and he passed away two weeks ago."

We talked for a few moments, all the while the female mouth with feet was standing there listening to our conversation.

I said, "Somewhere down the line we are probably related, but it would be a real sad thing if I didn't introduce you to the most important Person in my life." And—this just frosted my cake—he looked at that woman standing beside me as if I were talking about her. Well, I quickly cleared up that mistake!

Bob Hamblin was saved right there on that parking lot, and that woman just stood there watching, although she had quieted down.

We need to leave alone the priority of the landmark of soul winning, because it works.

Show me a church that always wants to defend the Faith but does not go soul winning, and I'll show you a church that has spiritual rigor mortis. In ten years that church will be able to fit all its members into a phone booth.

Unless a church, or a Christian, proclaims the Gospel while defending the Faith, it's not being done God's way.

The kind of fundamentalism I give to my children—and someday my grandchildren and my great-grandchildren—is the kind that I practice and protect.

What kind of fundamentalism will those after you find? It all rests on what we do with the old spiritual property lines, on whether or not we have moved the landmarks or kept them in place.

We have seen from the pages of the Bible that God said, "Remove not the ancient landmark, which thy fathers have set." Leave in place the landmarks of the perfect Scriptures, the precious Son of God and the priority of soul winning! Don't move them! Don't monkey with them!

One of the must-see places in Washington, D.C., is the Tomb of the Unknown Soldier in Arlington National Cemetery. This grave site represents all of the unidentified men and women who died for our country in the line of duty. An armed sentinel marches back and forth constantly in front of the tomb. When his watch is up, another comes to take his place. As the new soldier takes over, he is given these words from the departing guard: "Orders remain as directed."

Day after day, month after month, year after year, the orders to guard the tomb of the unknown soldier remain in effect as they were first given.

Just before the Lord Jesus Christ ascended into Heaven, He said "Go ye into all the world, and preach the gospel to every creature" (Mark 16:15). Those orders have never been altered or rescinded.

If you bend your ear toward Heaven right now, I'm sure you will hear Him saying, "Orders remain unchanged!" Don't change the landmarks! God set them there! Don't touch them!

Chapter 3

WHY THE BELIEVER
SHOULD BE FILLED
WITH THE SPIRIT

The child of God who does not experience the scriptural fullness of the Holy Spirit's power will inevitably become weak, weary and spiritually worthless. An automobile must have fuel in its tank to operate. In like manner, a Christian must be filled by the Holy Spirit to function.

"And be not drunk with wine, wherein is excess; but be filled with the Spirit."—Eph. 5:18.

There are several comparisons that we can make between a person who is filled with spirits and the person who is filled with the Spirit.

First, they are both under a power outside of themselves.

Second, they are both fervent. An example is the disciples on the day of Pentecost (Acts 2:13).

Third, they both have their walk affected.

Evangelist D. L. Moody penned in his personal Bible alongside Ephesians 5:18: "Two commands; both equally binding."

If you are saved, regardless of your station of service, God wants you to be filled with the Spirit. What great meetings we would have, what great ministries would be ours, if we had a fresh indwelling, a fresh empowerment, of the Spirit of God.

A preacher long ago said, "As a Christian you will be filled with the Spirit when the Holy Spirit who is the Resident of your heart becomes the President of your heart."

There are several scriptural, foundational, fundamental reasons why the believer should be filled with the Spirit.

I. TO BE AN ENERGIZED PREACHER

"And they [the disciples] were all filled with the Holy Ghost, and began to speak with other tongues, as the Spirit gave them utterance."—Acts 2:4.

They had come together for a season of prayer when God supernaturally placed His power upon them.

The apostle Peter preached a fiery sermon to a multitude of unbelievers after that Upper Room experience. "Peter, standing up with the eleven, lifted up his voice, and said unto them, Ye men of Judæa, and all ye that dwell at Jerusalem, be this known unto you, and hearken to my words" (vs. 14).

Peter "lifted up his voice." That tells us that he was a loud, wide-open preacher. Every preacher ought to lift up his voice when he preaches. Preaching is not teaching a Sunday school lesson; it's not a Wednesday night devotional. At preaching time a preacher ought to open the Word of God, rear back and let it fly.

"But if I get loud like Peter, people will get upset!" It's not the volume of the preacher that bothers most people; it's what he says that bothers them. It has little to do with decibels or the sound level, but it has everything to do with what he is saying and what he is preaching from the Word of God.

In one of my revival meetings, a lady on the back pew placed her hands over both ears and sat like that through the entire service. When I finished preaching, she came up to me and said, "Well, one thing's for sure: I heard every word that you said." Then she turned and walked away.

What she intended as a criticism, I accepted as a compliment. Even though she covered her ears, still she heard the Word of God that was preached.

Someone recently said to me, "Right in the middle of your sermon, the batteries in my hearing aid went dead, but I still heard every single word."

I like to lift up my voice with the Word of God!

The text of Peter's sermon was Joel, chapter 2:

"And it shall come to pass afterward, that I will pour out my spirit upon all flesh; and your sons and your daughters shall prophesy, your old men shall dream dreams, your young men shall see visions:

"And also upon the servants and upon the handmaids in those days will I pour out my spirit.

"And I will shew wonders in the heavens and in the earth, blood, and fire, and pillars of smoke.

"The sun shall be turned into darkness, and the moon into blood, before the great and terrible day of the LORD come.

"And it shall come to pass, that whosoever shall call on the name of the LORD shall be delivered: for in mount Zion and in Jerusalem shall be deliverance, as the LORD hath said, and in the

remnant whom the LORD shall call."—vss. 28–32.

The theme of his message is that Jesus is the Messiah. When he gave the invitation, there were three thousand souls saved, baptized and added to the young church.

Make no mistake about it, Brother Peter was an energized preacher who "lifted up his voice."

The paramount need of this hour is not for educated, eloquent or excited preachers, but for preachers who are energized by the Spirit of God.

I am not against education. I have the honor of being a teacher and trustee at Midwestern Baptist College. But education is not the answer.

I am not against eloquence; I realize that words are tools. Preachers should be as clear and articulate as they can be. But eloquence is not the answer.

I am not against an excited preacher. I appreciate excitement in a preacher, however that is not the answer.

The answer is a Spirit-filled preacher who is energized in the work of God.

Pastors, evangelists and missionaries should seek the fullness of the Holy Spirit until they can truthfully say about their preaching what the great apostle Paul said about his preaching: "My speech and my preaching was not with enticing words of man's wisdom, but in demonstration of the Spirit and of power" (I Cor. 2:4).

When that takes place, we'll see more unbelievers saved and more believers strengthened under our pulpit ministries.

A pulpit ministry is one of the greatest ministries there is. Get rid of that overhead projector and just preach! Stop using props and just preach! Save those colored markers for marking your Bible and just preach! What would happen in our churches if preachers were filled with the Spirit of God and just preached? They would mount the pulpit with new enthusiasm and new excitement, realizing the highest hour of the church is when the Word of God is faithfully declared.

In a revival meeting I preached in Indiana, the pastor told me that the song leader had years before been the song leader for Dr. Ford Porter.

Later I was able to meet and fellowship with him. One of the first things I asked was, "What's the single thing that stands out in your mind about Dr. Porter?"

He said, "I was never in his presence, no matter what time of day or night, that I did not sense that he was filled with the Spirit of God."

That is exactly what we all need: to be filled with the Spirit of God to such a degree that others know we've been with God.

II. TO BE AN EFFECTIVE SOUL WINNER

"And when they had prayed, the place was shaken where they were assembled together; and they were all filled with the Holy Ghost, and they spake the word of God with boldness."— Acts 4:31.

The Sanhedrin had forbidden the believers to witness about the saving power of the Lord Jesus Christ. They came together as a group to pray for fearlessness, and their prayer was answered. Every one of them was filled with the Holy Spirit and given holy boldness.

"And with great power gave the apostles witness of the resurrection of the Lord Jesus: and great grace was upon them all."—vs. 33.

Many unbelievers were won to Christ as a result of their prayer, their power and their personal witness.

You don't have to read very far into the Book of Acts until you see people being saved. And it can all be traced to those who were filled with the Spirit of God on the day of Pentecost.

Mark it down: when a believer is filled with the Spirit of God, he will always be an effective soul winner. Boldness is not crudeness; it is confidence. The Spirit's filling is all about winning souls.

Dr. Bob Jones, Sr., once said, "If anyone ought to be a gentleman, it's a saved man. If anyone ought to be a lady, it's a saved woman."

Sometimes I think we've come to the place in some circles where they think that someone is a great preacher if he is rude and crude. God forbid! That's idiotic and a far cry from greatness!

Young preacher, don't you imitate someone like that or make him the example you follow! Be the opposite! Don't buy into the idea that an obnoxious, rabid preacher is a great preacher. If someone ought to have impeccable manners and character, it ought to be a child of God.

Christians ought to deal with people the way they want people to deal with them. The things you say and the things you do may make for great illustrations, but they don't make up for being filled with the Spirit of God or having the fruit of the Spirit, which is gentleness. Rudeness and crudeness do not line up with the Bible!

There are several notable things that ought to inspire a Christian to be bold.

1. We should be inspired by the example of the Saviour. "But, lo, he speaketh boldly, and they say nothing unto him" (John 7:26).

There is not one time that the Lord Jesus Christ ever watered down anything He had to say during His earthly ministry.

2. We should be inspired by the encouragement of the Holy Spirit. "And they were not able to resist the wisdom and the spirit by which he spake" (Acts 6:10).

When a believer is filled with the Spirit, other people will take notice of his firm speech.

3. We should be inspired by the exhortation of the Scriptures. "Be not afraid of their faces: for I am with thee to deliver thee, saith the LORD" (Jer. 1:8).

The Bible admonishes the most timid believer to be bold.

Oh, that every single believer would be inspired to be bold by the example of the Saviour, the encouragement of the Holy Spirit and the exhortation of the Scriptures!

I read the story of a man who worked in the baggage room of a large railroad station. He dropped a heavy parcel on his foot, and he began to curse. A little girl standing in the doorway cried out, "Please, mister, don't talk that way! Don't you know that God hears you?"

Her words gripped the man and convicted him of his sinfulness. Throughout the balance of the day and night, her question plagued him: "Don't you know that God hears you?" The bold witness of a little child filled with the Spirit became the turning point of his life. Within a few days, he cried out to God in faith and was converted.

III. TO BE AN EXEMPLARY CHRISTIAN

"Wherefore, brethren, look ye out among you seven men of honest report, full of the Holy Ghost and wisdom, whom we may appoint over this business."—Acts 6:3.

The apostles had recommended to the church at Jerusalem that seven men who were filled with the Holy Spirit be selected to serve the church. They were perhaps the very first deacons. These men were chosen from a spiritual pool of prospects and placed in a spiritual position.

That's the way it always ought to be, regardless of what position is to be filled in the church. We never ought to choose an unspiritual person and put him in a spiritual place. An unspiritual person will not become spiritual because of a position in which he has been placed. It is always disastrous for that person and for the one placing him in that position.

These seven men were spiritual men. One of them was Stephen. His name means "crown." He was a crown to the church and to the people. When he was picked to serve, the assembly at Jerusalem gained a helper with an outstanding reputation. "And Stephen, full of faith and power, did great wonders and miracles among the people" (vs. 8).

There is not one flaw we can find in Stephen's spiritual character. He served as a deacon, he was a preacher, and he was a soul winner. He was the soul winner who was primarily responsible for the conversion of Saul of Tarsus, the persecutor of Christians who later became the great Paul, a preacher for Christ and the apostle to the Gentiles.

We should desire to be filled with the Holy Spirit like dear Stephen, so that long after we are gone, our names will bring to mind a life that was lived for right, for good and for Christ.

Proverbs 22:1 says, "A good name is rather to be chosen than great riches, and loving favour rather than silver and gold."

Dr. R. G. Lee said, "When our garments have been moth-eaten, when our photographs have faded, when our house has been pulled down, when the grave has sunk as level as the road, our subtle image will remain in blackness or beauty, influencing posterity."

I believe the Lord could come at any moment—even before I finish this sermon—but if he doesn't, it ought to be our burning desire, our heart's longing, to maintain a legacy of spirituality that only comes when the believer is filled with the Holy Spirit. The end of your earthly life will not be the finish of your testimony.

Robert Ingersoll, an infamous atheist, hated God and the things of God; but he had an Aunt Sarah who was a devout Christian, a real Bible student. One day he sent her a book he had written. It was an attack on the Bible. On the inside flyleaf he had written, "If all Christians had lived like Aunt Sarah, perhaps this book would never have been written."

Isn't it amazing that it was the life of a Spirit-filled saint that caused a skeptic to put a question mark over all of his hellish doubts?

I don't want to be a hypocrite about any verse in the Bible, but if there's one about which I definitely don't want

31

to be a hypocrite, it's Ephesians 5:18: "And be not drunk with wine, wherein is excess; but be filled with the Spirit."

Why should the believer be filled with the Spirit? To be an energized preacher. Why? To be an effective soul winner. Why? To be an exemplary Christian.

Chapter 4

WHAT KEEPS ME FROM BLOWING THE BUGLE OF RETREAT?

*"And the L*ORD *spake unto Moses, saying,*

"Make thee two trumpets of silver; of a whole piece shalt thou make them: that thou mayest use them for the calling of the assembly, and for the journeying of the camps.

"And when they shall blow with them, all the assembly shall assemble themselves to thee at the door of the tabernacle of the congregation.

"And if they blow but with one trumpet, then the princes, which are heads of the thousands of Israel, shall gather themselves unto thee.

"When ye blow an alarm, then the camps that lie on the east parts shall go forward.

"When ye blow an alarm the second time, then the camps that lie on the south side shall take their journey: they shall blow an alarm for their journeys.

"But when the congregation is to be gathered together, ye shall blow, but ye shall not sound an alarm.

"And the sons of Aaron, the priests, shall blow with the

trumpets; and they shall be to you for an ordinance for ever throughout your generations.

"And if ye go to war in your land against the enemy that oppresseth you, then ye shall blow an alarm with the trumpets; and ye shall be remembered before the LORD your God, and ye shall be saved from your enemies.

"Also in the day of your gladness, and in your solemn days, and in the beginnings of your months, ye shall blow with the trumpets over your burnt-offerings, and over the sacrifices of your peace-offerings; that they may be to you for a memorial before your God: I am the LORD your God."—Num. 10:1–10.

In many places today the work of God suffers instead of succeeding because a large number of believers have the trumpet raised to their lips and are ready to play "I'm Turning Back." When truly born-again Christians begin playing such heartbreaking notes, it will not be long before they give up on their ministry and perhaps their marriage and others of the most important things in life.

Moses, under the direct inspiration of the Holy Spirit, tells us (vs. 2) that there are only two occasions when the children of Israel were authorized to blow the attention-commanding trumpets. One time was for the calling of the assembly.

One of the greatest callings for assembly is found in I Thessalonians 4:16 and 17:

"For the Lord himself shall descend from heaven with a shout, with the voice of the archangel, and with the trump [trumpet] *of God: and the dead in Christ shall rise first:*

"Then we which are alive and remain shall be caught up

together with them in the clouds, to meet the Lord in the air: and so shall we ever be with the Lord."

The second call was for the journeying of the camp.

G. Campbell Morgan wrote, "The use of trumpets in the history of the people of Israel is full of interest, and here we find instructions concerning it. The trumpets were intended to call the people to attention so they would be led to obedience. For the people, the blast of the trumpet was always as authoritative as the voice of God."

Never was the trumpet intended to cause the children of Israel to pull back, but only to push ahead. Every Christian should have something sufficient in his soul that keeps him from blowing the bugle of retreat.

There are few days that pass that I don't hear of some Christian who has given up and turned back. Every one of us at one time or another has thought about quitting, but we must not turn back or turn aside.

I want to give you three things that keep me from blowing the bugle of retreat.

I. THE CROSS

"And he bearing his cross went forth into a place called the place of a skull, which is called in the Hebrew Golgotha."—John 19:17.

The Lord Jesus Christ carried His cross—that age-old symbol of redemption—outside the city of Jerusalem and up to the raised piece of rocky earth called Golgotha.

This mountain received its heart-wrenching name because "Golgotha" means "skull" and the hill itself resembled the head of a human skeleton, and it was the place where criminals were executed. It is likely that there were bleached skulls and bones scattered about the area.

The songwriter, George Bennard, must have had this truth upon his heart as he wrote "The Old Rugged Cross":

On a hill far away stood an old rugged cross,
The emblem of suff'ring and shame;
And I love that old cross where the dearest and best
For a world of lost sinners was slain.

Friends, we should not blow the bugle of retreat because of the cross.

Galatians 6:14 says, "God forbid that I should glory, save in the cross of our Lord Jesus Christ."

Every conceivable reason that the Christian utters for giving up is clearly refuted and dealt with under or near the cross of Calvary.

You want to quit because someone betrayed you. Come near to the cross and hear: "And forthwith he [Judas] came to Jesus, and said, Hail, master; and kissed him" (Matt. 26:49).

You want to stop serving the Lord because you feel unappreciated? Come near to the cross and hear these words: "They crucified him, and parted his garments, casting lots" (Matt. 27:35).

You complain because someone spoke rudely to you? Come near the cross and hear:

"The chief priests mocking him, with the scribes and elders, said,

"He saved others; himself he cannot save. If he be the King of Israel, let him now come down from the cross, and we will believe him.

"He trusted in God; let him deliver him now, if he will have

him: for he said, I am the Son of God.

"The thieves also, which were crucified with him, cast the same in his teeth."—Matt. 27:41–44.

How can you quit when you think about the cross? How can you give up when you think about Calvary? How do you turn back when you think about Jesus on Golgotha?

No Christian would ever give serious consideration to signing a letter of resignation from God's service if he would just remember his Saviour on Mount Calvary.

A Christian man from the Philippines told of an experience he had on the day that some call Good Friday. He noticed a crowd around a certain church—not only worshipers, but many vendors selling incense, candles, veils and rosaries had gathered. Mingling among that crowd were boys calling out, "Get your cheap crosses here!"

What he heard expressed meaning beyond its intent, and he thought, *Some people like an easy religion, one that is all sweetness and that makes no demands upon their interests or claims upon their time and strength. To them, the cross actually came in a cheap manner!*

If you keep upon your heart the truth that Heaven paid a major price so people on earth would know what it is to be born again, then you'll understand that there is no such thing as a cheap cross, and you'll never succumb to the temptation to blow the bugle of retreat!

II. THE COMMISSION

"And he said unto them, Go ye into all the world, and preach the gospel to every creature."—Mark 16:15.

Before the Lord Jesus ascended into Heaven, He purposely gave the eleven disciples their lifelong responsibility—the task of world evangelization.

Dr. Shelton Smith has said, "The scriptural mandate of Christ's great commission is color-blind and seven continents wide."

How can you think of blowing the bugle of retreat when you're trying to keep people out of Hell? How can you quit when you're trying to take people with you to Heaven? How can you turn aside when you're trying to get out the Good News of the Gospel? Quitting and keeping the Great Commission are an impossible match! They simply do not go together!

The believer who attempts to fulfill the Saviour's witnessing assignment will have several distinguishing characteristics.

1. He is obedient. "He arose and went" (Acts 8:27).

At the end of the road of soul-winning obedience, you'll always find a reachable soul.

The pastor of Calvary Baptist Church in Manistee, Michigan was telling me that every week for the past several months folks have been saved through the outreach of the church.

It works when you are obedient.

I was talking to a young man this week who is a very strong and fervent witness. I had gone to a local store to buy some things, and this young man said to me, "I just got my first brand-new car."

I said, "I'll bet you're a tither."

"Yes, I am, and God is blessing me like I've never been

38

blessed before." And, brother, we had us a camp meeting right there in the store!

Whether it is tithing, soul winning or prayer, if you do your part, God will do His part.

2. He is outgoing. "And the lord said unto the servant, Go out into the highways and hedges, and compel them to come in, that my house may be filled" (Luke 14:23).

An obedient witness is always going out after people. Why? Because most times you won't find sinners in the pews or parlors of the church, but in the highways and hedges of the world.

There is no mystery or marvel that the church in Manistee has been growing. Last year they had a soul-winning blitz on the surrounding area; as a result of their soul-winning obedience, folks were saved. God blesses when His people do as ordered. When we get up, get out, and get going, God blesses! That's just the way it is! That's the way it's supposed to be!

3. He is overjoyed. "He that goeth forth and weepeth, bearing precious seed, shall doubtless come again with rejoicing, bringing his sheaves with him" (Ps. 126:6).

Soul-winning Christians make the best church members. They enjoy nothing better than seeing people saved. Consequently, they smile! They sing! They shout!

Several weeks ago a man from my church drove with me to West Virginia. We stopped at an all-night doughnut shop. The people behind the counter were both from India, and after we got our order, I gave them a gospel tract and started to walk away. But God wouldn't untie my heart, so I turned back, and in less time than it takes for me to tell it, they were born into the family of God.

Not an hour went by when that man and I didn't smile and sing and shout out loud about what had happened. In fact, we kept at it hour after hour as we drove. It seemed as though we floated down the highway to West Virginia.

Soul winners make shouters.

If you don't get excited and shout once in a while, maybe it's because you've never told anyone about Jesus. When folks get saved and others get excited and you're not excited, maybe it's because you are not involved in seeing anybody saved.

Soul winners are overjoyed, and they shout it out!

Oh, that every one of us would realize the wonderful things that can be accurately said about the believer who attempts to fulfill the soul-winning assignment—that they are obedient; they are outgoing; they are overjoyed!

Early one morning a timid knock came at London's No. 10 Downing Street (the equivalent of knocking on the White House door). William Gladstone, one of England's greatest prime ministers, was working on a speech he was supposed to deliver that day in Parliament. He left his desk to answer the door and found a little boy whose friendship Prime Minister Gladstone had won by little deeds of kindness.

With tears in his eyes, the child said, "Mr. Gladstone, would you come? My brother is dying, and would you please show him the way to Heaven?"

Prime Minister Gladstone left his important work for the most important work in which a Christian can ever be involved. He went to the bedside of that dying boy, and in a matter of moments the child was rejoicing in his new-found Saviour.

Returning to his desk, the prime minister picked up his pen and wrote on the bottom of his speech, "I am the happiest man in London today!"

When the Commission keeps you from turning back and you win someone to the Saviour, you too will be the happiest person in your town!

III. THE COMMENDATION

"For we must all appear before the judgment seat of Christ; that every one may receive the things done in his body, according to that he hath done, whether it be good or bad."—II Cor. 5:10.

Not only will the cross and the commission keep us from blowing the bugle of retreat, but the commendation will as well.

Commendation means "that which presents a person or a thing to another in a favorable light and renders them worthy of regard or reward."

After the rapture, every Christian is going to stand at the judgment seat of Christ (*bema* in the Greek) to have the amount, the quality and the motive of his service examined.

This will not be an appraisal of one's salvation, but an assessment of one's service. You don't get to the judgment seat to find out whether or not you are saved; you get there because you are saved.

At the bema seat there are five crowns that may be given as rewards to a believer.

First, there is the crown of life. This is the martyr's garland. "Blessed is the man that endureth temptation: for when he is tried, he shall receive the crown of life, which the

41

Lord hath promised to them that love him" (Jas. 1:12).

Next, there is the crown of glory. This is the preacher's garland. "And when the chief Shepherd shall appear, ye [the elders, or preachers] shall receive a crown of glory that fadeth not away" (I Pet. 5:4).

Then we can win the crown of rejoicing. This is the soul winner's garland. "What is our hope, or joy, or crown of rejoicing?...For ye are our glory and joy" (I Thess. 2:19, 20).

Also, there is the crown of righteousness. This is the rapturous garland. "Henceforth there is laid up for me a crown of righteousness, which the Lord, the righteous judge, shall give me at that day: and not to me only, but unto all them also that love his appearing" (II Tim. 4:8).

Fifth, we should strive for the crown of moral integrity. This is the separatist's garland. "Every man that striveth for the mastery is temperate in all things. Now they do it to obtain a corruptible crown; but we an incorruptible" (I Cor. 9:25).

These crowns will be presented to believers who have earned them. The Bible says, "Look to yourselves, that we lose not those things which we have wrought, but that we receive a full reward" (II John 8).

If a Christian who has served God faithfully for many years throws in the towel today and the rapture takes place tomorrow, he will not "receive a full reward." It's more than sufficient reason to stay faithful. We should not blow the bugle of retreat because of the commendation!

On a recent flight to Canada, I struck up a conversation with the man seated next to me. I gave him a gospel tract and asked him to read it. He flipped down the tray in front of him and read every word on the front and back, closed it, patted it, then said, "I did that when I was seven down in Georgia, and I got saved."

Since he knew I had written the tract, he asked me to autograph it. Then he told me he was on his way to compete in an international track-and-field event. In fact, he humbly told me that he had been part of a four-by-four-hundred-meter relay team that won a gold medal for the USA in Sydney. Then I asked him for his autograph, and he pulled out a publicity picture and signed it.

We talked about his training and his mental preparation before a race. I pulled out a pad of legal paper and started writing down his answers.

Question: "What goes through your mind before the starting gun goes off?"

Answer: "I think about how this is my race to win or it is my race to lose. I don't think about the person in the lane to the left or the person to the right; I just think about me in my lane."

If Christians were as concerned about ourselves as we are unnecessarily about everyone else, we'd be better Christians.

Question: "What is it like to stand on the pedestal when that gold medal is hung around your neck?"

Answer: "I was looking for my mother and coaches in the arena." Then with tears in his eyes, he said, "That really wasn't my medal. It belonged to my parents, my wife, my coaches, my high-school teachers and the prayer warriors who prayed for me."

This gold-medal winner was a Christian who was unashamed to give credit to those who influenced his life behind the scenes.

FIRE IN THE PULPIT

When we believers, the sainted servants of God, stand on the pedestal of Heaven, we will look full into the face of Jesus; it's likely we'll also look toward the glorious grandstand for those who have impacted and influenced our lives.

I don't know anyone who loves preachers and their work for the Lord more than my beloved mother. There are churches that sit on paid-for property, Bible college students who do not have a school bill, preachers and their wives who wear new clothes, and missionaries on the mission field because of her generosity. If I receive a crown, I will be searching Glory's grandstand looking for my mother.

Sometimes I preach as often as five times a day; but no matter where I am or how often I preach, I always get a call from my mother who tells me, "Son, I want you to know that I'm praying for you and that meeting. Before you get to that pulpit, rest assured that I've held you up to God."

I'll look for my precious wife, Cari. We've been married twenty years, and God has blessed us. I was an evangelist when we were dating, I was an evangelist when we got married, I have been an evangelist every day we've been married, and not once—not ever—has she uttered a negative word about my being an evangelist.

It's difficult to be an evangelist's wife. She is a pew widow, meaning that she sits in our home church by herself almost every service. By herself, she must deal with household problems—broken garbage disposals, unshoveled driveways and sidewalks, etc.

When I'm away and call home, she always asks how my meetings are going. Before she hangs up, she says, "I'm praying for you and the services."

There are so many others who have been a blessing in my life, and I'll be looking for them too.

Often the preacher and the evangelist are away from home by themselves, and they need good people in their corner, good people praying for them and encouraging them and helping them. When those preachers or evangelists get on the heavenly pedestal, wouldn't you like to be one of the ones they're looking for?

Sometime in your Christian life, you're going to think about giving up, turning back, turning aside and blowing the bugle of retreat! Don't do it! When that sad day dawns, go back to the hour of your salvation when you found the reasons for marching forward and not retreating.

No believer should have on his spiritual music stand the sheet music for "Fall Back." Instead, begin to play and sing "Onward, Christian Soldiers."

In discouragement, don't blow the bugle of retreat.

In disappointment, don't blow the bugle of retreat.

In defeat, don't blow the bugle of retreat.

In a crisis, don't blow the bugle of retreat.

At the crash, don't blow the bugle of retreat.

Off the course, don't blow the bugle of retreat.

When under fire, don't blow the bugle of retreat.

When underfunded, don't blow the bugle of retreat.

When under fear, don't blow the bugle of retreat.

No matter what! No matter who! No matter when! No matter why!

Don't roll over! Don't resign! Don't retreat!

Chapter 5

"DAILY"

"And they, continuing daily with one accord in the temple, and breaking bread from house to house, did eat their meat with gladness and singleness of heart,

"Praising God, and having favour with all the people. And the Lord added to the church daily such as should be saved."— Acts 2:46, 47.

The believer's lack of powerful influence in today's world is a major problem. It is primarily a matter of living by a wrong philosophy. If Christianity is something that an individual practices only one day a week, it is not a biblical faith at all. That may be "churchianity," but it is certainly not Christianity.

The moment a Christian decides to walk with God "daily," his life will immediately assume a new and distinctive character.

The word *daily* is used nine times in the Book of Acts. It simply refers to "the time space between dawn and dark."

If today's believers would place on their "daily" calendars what the first-century believers practiced, they would quickly discover first-century power. From dark till dawn and from dawn till dark, the claims of Christ should have a position, a prominence and a priority.

Christians should not let a single day pass without having accomplished certain spiritual assignments. Let me suggest three things each of God's children should be doing every day.

I. "DAILY" SUPPLICATION

"And they, continuing daily with one accord in the temple, and breaking bread from house to house, did eat their meat with gladness and singleness of heart."—Vs. 46.

The believers in the early church placed a strong emphasis upon prayer. They were "daily" in the temple, and Acts 3:1 tells us when they went:

"Now Peter and John went up together into the temple at the hour of prayer, being the ninth hour."

There were three distinct prayer times in the temple: nine o'clock in the morning, at noon and at three o'clock in the afternoon. Peter and John, two very influential individuals, filled their day with prayer because prayer was paramount in their lives.

Ralph Cushman wrote these moving words:

> **I met God in the morning,**
>   **When the day was at its best;**
> **And His presence came like sunrise,**
>   **Like a glory in my breast.**
>
> **All day long His presence lingered,**
>   **All day long He stayed with me,**
> **And we sailed in perfect calmness**
>   **O'er a very troubled sea.**
>
> **Other ships were blown and battered,**
>   **Other ships were sore distressed,**

48

But the winds that seemed to drive them
   Brought to me a peace and rest.

Then I thought of other mornings,
   With a keen remorse of mind,
When I too had loosed the moorings
   With His presence left behind.

So I think I know the secret,
   Learned from many a troubled way;
You must seek him in the morning
   If you want Him through the day!

We ought to be found "daily" looking to God in supplication.

Psalm 38:9 says, "Lord, all my desire is before thee; and my groaning is not hid from thee."

No twenty-four-hour period should pass when Heaven does not hear our earnest requests for the names and needs on our prayer lists. Our lists may have some requests in common, but most of our lists have names and needs on them that aren't on anyone else's. If we don't pray for them, nobody else will either.

I watched with great interest when President George W. Bush marked his one hundredth day in office. He told the reporter, "I am on bended knee every morning, asking for guidance and comfort." How refreshing! I remember the times when it was not that way at the White House! I tip my hat to a president who is interested more in intercession than he is in interns. I am glad for a president who starts every day talking to God and gaining the ear of the Lord!

One night a British soldier was caught creeping stealthily from his quarters to a nearby woods. He was taken before his commanding officer and charged with holding communications with the enemy. The man pleaded that he had gone into the woods to pray by himself. That was his only defense.

"Have you been in the habit of spending hours in private prayer?" the officer growled.

"Yes sir!"

"Then down on your knees and pray now!" he roared. "You've never needed it so much."

Expecting immediate death, the soldier knelt and poured out his soul in prayer.

When he was through, the officer said, "You may go. I believe your story. If you hadn't drilled so often, you could not have done so well at review."

If you were given a microphone tonight in this service and asked to pray, how would you do in review?

II. "DAILY" STUDYING THE SCRIPTURES

"These were more noble than those in Thessalonica, in that they received the word with all readiness of mind, and searched the scriptures daily, whether those things were so."—Acts 17:11.

The believers in the early church placed a strong emphasis upon practical Bible study. They wanted to make sure that what they were learning and how they were living lined up with the Word of God.

Christians today should make sure that every day they're found by God doing their spiritual assignment, that they are studying the Scriptures.

The Bible is not an accessory that fundamental

Christians with a sharp-looking, four-button suit or a long, elegant dress carry. The Bible is to be our all, our everything and our blueprint.

The exploration of the Bible will do several exciting things for a believer.

1. It will inspire hope. "Remember the word unto thy servant, upon which thou hast caused me to hope" (Ps. 119:49).

It is impossible for a person to peruse the pages of the Word of God and be a spiritual pessimist. Show me a Christian with a negative attitude, who thinks every day is doomsday, and I'll show you a Christian who hasn't been in the Bible in a long time. Show me a Christian whose lips drag low on the ground like a vacuum cleaner, and I'll show you a Christian with dust on his Bible.

2. It will inaugurate happiness. "The statutes of the LORD are right, rejoicing the heart" (Ps. 19:8).

A Bible reader is a rejoicing believer. There are certain folks in some of our churches who would be disgruntled if Paul was their pastor, John the Baptist held a revival meeting and David led the choir—because they're not reading the Bible.

Those who read the Bible have a smile on their face, a song in their heart, a spring in their step; and they will not look like they've been baptized in embalming fluid!

Some Christians enjoy their Christianity; others only endure it. Reading the Bible "daily" brings you happiness. It is a joy to be around Christians who embrace the things of the Lord because they read their Bible.

There is nothing better than knowing that you are saved,

that the Lord is Master in your life, that Heaven is your home and that the rapture may occur at any moment! We'll hear a toot, and then we'll scoot! We'll hear a shout, and then we're out! We'll hear a trump, and then we'll jump! What's better than that?

If you don't read your Bible, you'll be upset and irritated about everything.

3. It will instigate a holy heartburn. "And they said one to another, Did not our heart burn within us, while he talked with us by the way, and while he opened to us the scriptures?" (Luke 24:32).

The glowing fire of revival will never burn in a church until Scripture reading is done with intensity by the servants of God.

John Wanamaker, one of the country's greatest merchants in the nineteenth century, said:

> I have of course made large purchases of property in my lifetime, and the buildings and ground in which we are now meeting represent a value of approximately twenty million dollars. But it was as a boy in the country, at eleven years of age, in a little missions Sunday school, that I made my biggest purchase. I bought from my teacher a small, red, leather Bible. The Bible cost me $2.75, which I paid in small installments as I saved.
>
> This was my greatest purchase, for the Bible made me what I am today.

After that statement, the *New York Herald Tribune* captioned its write-up thus:

> Later deals in millions called small compared with

buying Holy Writ at eleven.

The Christians who know that the Bible was their greatest purchase are those who never let a day pass without reading the Word of God.

III. "DAILY" SOUL WINNING

"And daily in the temple, and in every house, they ceased not to teach and preach Jesus Christ."—Acts 5:42.

Read the Book of Acts! Read all of it! Read it again! You will discover that the believers in the early church placed a strong emphasis upon pointing people to the Saviour.

When I look at this altar, I think about all the years that people have been coming here and hearing the Word of God, receiving the Gospel and being won to the Lord Jesus Christ. Oh, how we could fill this auditorium innumerable times with people whose lives have been redeemed and rescued because God is in the soul-saving business.

Dr. John R. Rice said about Acts 5:42, "Every Christian, a preacher; every house, a church; every gathering, a congregation to hear the Gospel; every incident that occurs, another occasion to draw men to Christ."

When a person keeps the effort of Acts 5:42 in mind, it is no surprise that the effect of Acts 6:1 follows in its great wake: "And in those days, when the number of the disciples was multiplied...."

If you want disciples to increase in number, surging and growing, then the answer is in "daily" witnessing.

We should be engaged "daily" in soul winning. Mark 16:15 says, "And he said unto them, Go ye into all the world, and preach the gospel to every creature."

Carrying out the Great Commission was never intended to be done only on Thursday nights or Saturday mornings. It's something we ought to be doing every day—"daily."

You may see someone today that you won't ever see again, so if you wait until a specified day, you may lose the opportunity to see that person saved.

When I'm out of town, I meet folks that I'll probably not ever see again—at the gas station and grocery store, in the airport, even on the street—and I can't wait until a specified time to give them the Gospel; I do it then either by personally witnessing to them or by putting a gospel tract in their hands.

Sometime ago my wife and I went out to dinner with a group from our church. After having a delicious meal, we went to an outlet mall. I found a mannequin in one of the shops, and I put a gospel tract in its hand. A member of our group walked up to me and said, "Look at that! Even dummies can pass out gospel tracts!"

I saw this happen in church recently. A little four-year-old girl saw people at the altar. When she asked her mother what they were doing, her mother replied, "Some are asking Jesus to save them now."

The little girl said, "Mommy, I need to do that too."

They walked down the aisle and knelt at the altar. The mother took an open Bible and led her daughter to the Lord. Mother didn't wait for a specified time; instead, she witnessed when the opportunity arose, and the little girl accepted Jesus Christ as her Saviour.

Such is "daily" witnessing for the Lord.

I have three hobbies. I like to golf, and I made a resolution that I would go golfing more this summer than ever before. The count is now at two. I'm burning up the greens.

Another hobby is collecting quaint and unique sayings on church marquees. Three of my favorites are "Here no bingo, just Bible," "God Answers Knee Mail" and "To belittle is to be little."

My third hobby is collecting fine, expensive "signing" pens. Pentel pens, once imported from Japan, flooded the market in the United States when I was a teenager in high school. I bought one of the first ones that came out. In one year's time sales had climbed to $1.8 million—and that without heavy promotion, only word-of-mouth advertising.

Can you imagine the number of people who would be brought to a saving knowledge of the Lord Jesus Christ if we just talked about Him the way people talked about that brand of pen!

God should find us in "daily" supplication, "daily" studying of the Scriptures and "daily" soul winning.

Chapter 6

FLIGHT 93

On September 11, 2002, America marked the first anniversary of the terrorist attack upon our nation. Within days of that awful, infamous event, I personally visited all of the sights where the terrorists did their destructive deeds.

On September 18, 2001, one week to the day after the attacks, I stood beside the Pentagon. I saw the massive building so badly devastated. A number of the bodies had not yet been recovered.

On October 11, one month to the day, I was but four miles from where the plane crashed in Shanksville, Pennsylvania.

On October 23, six weeks to the day, I stood one-half block from Ground Zero in New York where the fires were still burning and the smoke still lazily billowing up into the sky.

At each of the three sites I grieved. My heart hurt. I was moved with deep emotions.

"Bless the LORD, O my soul. O LORD my God, thou art very great; thou art clothed with honour and majesty.

"Who coverest thyself with light as with a garment: who stretchest out the heavens like a curtain:

"Who layeth the beams of his chambers in the waters: who maketh the clouds his chariot: who walketh upon the wings of the wind:

"Who maketh his angels spirits; his ministers a flaming fire:

"Who laid the foundations of the earth, that it should not be removed for ever.

"Thou coveredst it with the deep as with a garment: the waters stood above the mountains.

"At thy rebuke they fled; at the voice of thy thunder they hasted away.

"They go up by the mountains; they go down by the valleys unto the place which thou hast founded for them.

"Thou hast set a bound that they may not pass over; that they turn not again to cover the earth."—Ps. 104:1–9.

On that fateful morning, America experienced what many have referred to as "the second Pearl Harbor." It is itself a day that will forever stand unforgettable in its sorrowful significance.

Although tragedy seemed to claim the day, from the ashes of the charred crater in Shanksville, Pennsylvania there came an amazing story of triumph.

Verse 3 contains a profound phrase: "who walketh upon the wings of the wind." There is a sister verse to this one in II Samuel 22:11: "And he [God] was seen upon the wings of the wind."

On board Flight 93, this scheduled transcontinental flight of 9/11, I believe the God who created the universe crafted a living parable, a profound message for the land of the free and the home of the brave.

Some things transpired and some things were said in the final moments of that fateful flight which bear the fingerprints of Almighty God.

58

There are three powerful truths that make their way from the Shanksville crater to the soul of the country.

I. FAITH MATTERS

"Jesus answering saith unto them, Have faith in God."— Mark 11:22.

While looking at a fig tree that had withered from the roots up, the Lord Jesus Christ said to His small band of followers, "Have faith in God."

What does a dried up tree have to do with a dependence on Deity? If one has faith in God, he can deal with the problem of fruitlessness that will always pop up in his spiritual path.

This simple four-word phrase is the unfailing answer to every problem, peril or predicament. No person among us will ever find himself up against a dilemma so dire that the Lord God of Heaven cannot deliver.

Just a short while ago a dear man shared with me some things in his life that would make a stone weep. I said what I could say to encourage him, and I prayed with him, but the solution to his problem, as is the case with every problem, is "faith in God."

The Bible says, "So then faith cometh by hearing, and hearing by the word of God" (Rom. 10:17).

When the child of God feels that his dependence on God is small or shrinking, the place he should go is directly to the Word of God.

I often think about fundamental Christians who come to church on Sunday morning, Sunday night and Wednesday night with a myriad of problems and do not realize that the answer they seek is right in the Book they hold in their hands.

There is nothing you face, nothing that opposes you, nothing you are going through that doesn't find an answer, a remedy, in the sixty-six books of the Holy Writ of God, the King James Bible!

Todd Beamer, a Christian man, a Sunday school teacher from New Jersey, was a passenger on Flight 93 on 9/11. He may have been experiencing difficulty with his credit card, for his call at 9:45 A.M. was routed to the GTE Customer Service Center in Oak Brook, Illinois.

He told an operator/supervisor, Mrs. Lisa Jefferson, that their flight had been hijacked. In a businesslike way, he told her that there were three hijackers, two of which had knives, ten passengers in first class, twenty-seven in coach, five flight attendants, no children that he could see, and that a flight attendant had told him that the captain and first officer were lying dead on the floor in first class.

"Lisa?" he said suddenly.

"Yes," Mrs. Jefferson said.

"That's my wife's name." Then he said, "I don't think we are going to get out of this thing. I'm going to have to go out on faith."

He then asked Mrs. Jefferson to recite with him what is commonly referred to as "The Lord's Prayer." Over that phone, they said together:

"Our Father which art in heaven, Hallowed be thy name.

"Thy kingdom come. Thy will be done in earth, as it is in heaven.

"Give us this day our daily bread.

"And forgive us our debts, as we forgive our debtors.

"And lead us not into temptation, but deliver us from evil: For thine is the kingdom, and the power, and the glory, for ever. Amen."—Matt. 6:9–13.

Isn't it amazing that at the moment of this high altitude trauma 30,000 feet above the earth, soaring at over 500 mph, Todd Beamer, looking Death in the eye, drew his strength from the Word of God and his solace from the will of God?

This type of faith is not to be held in reserve for catastrophic situations; it should be always at ready for everyday, common scenarios.

II. FAMILY MATTERS

"Lo, children are an heritage of the LORD*: and the fruit of the womb is his reward."*—Ps. 127:3.

Children are a gift from God. Children who are brought up in the discipline and the instruction of the Lord are a wonderful "reward" to a father and mother.

God has always desired to place His hand of blessing upon the family in which He can find delight.

With babies being aborted in butcher shops called abortion clinics, America needs to know that family matters. With hardly a moment going by without another home being broken by divorce, America needs to know that family matters.

With couples moving in together and playing house before taking their wedding vows and receiving the blessing of God upon their lives, America needs to know that family matters.

With the insane idea that two homosexual men make a home or that two lesbian women make a home, America needs to know that family, according to God's plan, matters.

There are several important things that Christian parents must do for their children. Even if you have a broken home and you are left to rear your children alone, if you will just be a godly parent, God can enable you to pick up the spiritual slack.

1. Cherish your children. "And he [the Prodigal Son] arose, and came to his father. But when he was yet a great way off, his father saw him, and had compassion, and ran, and fell on his neck, and kissed him" (Luke 15:20).

It is necessary, it is a requirement, that parents should cherish their children. The time to start teaching them is not after they've left the hogpen but before they leave the homeplace.

Have you kissed your children today? Even if they are out on their own, living two states away, you can blow them a kiss long distance over the phone.

I have two teenagers under my roof, and they do not like public affection. But I give them public affection because if Jesus stays His coming and they are one day standing by Dad's open grave, they will know that Dad loved them and wasn't ashamed to be affectionate.

Cherish your children.

2. Correct your children. "Withhold not correction from the child" (Prov. 23:13).

Biblical correction is always proper and beneficial to the children. You cannot improve the Bible way, and its way is to correct them.

Dr. Bob Jones, Sr., said, "You ought to beat your kids every day. You may not know why, but they'll know why."

Correct your children.

3. Challenge your children. "Provoke not your children to wrath: but bring them up in the nurture and admonition of the Lord" (Eph. 6:4).

The number one priority of parents is to put before their children a proper pattern of godly living. If parents don't read their Bible, it's unlikely the children will read their Bible. If parents don't have a prayer life, it is unlikely the children will have a prayer life. If parents don't faithfully attend God's house, it is unlikely the children will regularly attend church.

Challenge your children.

Every parent needs to cherish, correct and challenge his or her children.

When the harsh reality of 9/11 became clear to the passengers and flight attendants on Flight 93, they began to use the cell phones to contact their loved ones. Passenger Jeremy Glick called his wife and told her that the plane had been hijacked and that the hijackers had told them they had a bomb. Mrs. Glick started to panic, but her husband calmed her, and for several minutes husband and wife said "I love you" over and over again.

Then Mr. Glick told his wife how important it was for her and their little girl to be happy and that he would respect any decision she had to make in the days ahead.

Flight Attendant C. C. Lyles called her husband, Lawrence, and said, "My plane has been hijacked." Then they talked about their love and their four boys.

Passenger Lauren Grandcolas left a message for her husband on the answering machine: "There's been a little problem. I'm fine and comfortable for now. I'll call—" Then she stopped herself and told him how much she loved him and their family. Those were her last recorded words.

Christian, ere this night is over, you gather your close relations around you, look them in the eye and say, "Outside of God, you are more important than anything on this planet to me!"

Family matters.

III. FORTITUDE MATTERS

"Watch ye, stand fast in the faith, quit you like men, be strong."—I Cor. 16:13.

Courage in the face of crisis matters. The duty of Christians, no matter the day or the dilemma in which they find themselves, is to be strong and not to quit.

The word fortitude means "that strength or firmness of mind or soul which enables a person to encounter danger with coolness and courage."

The Bible says we are to "fight the good fight of faith" (I Tim. 6:12).

Between 9:30 A.M. and 9:45 A.M., all the passengers and attendants on Flight 93 were herded to the back of the plane. Flight Attendant Sandy Bradshaw told her husband, Phil, on the phone that she was in the coach class galley with other flight attendants filling coffee pots with boiling water to throw at the hijackers.

Jeremy Glick told his wife that the passengers were taking a vote on what to do. (There must not have been any Baptists on that flight because they actually did something after a vote!) He shared with her in a joking manner, "I've got my butter knife from breakfast."

The spirit of America! What an example of what we are all about, what that red, white and blue stands for! Americans standing! Americans smiling in the face of death!

Todd Beamer told Lisa Jefferson that the passengers were going to try to jump the hijackers.

"Are you sure that's what you want to do, Todd?" she asked.

His steely response was, "It's what we have to do!"

After praying with Mr. Beamer, Mrs. Jefferson heard him recite Psalm 23 with nearby passengers. Then he put down the phone and said those words which now live forever with other great statements in American history: "Let's roll!"

The distance on a Boeing 757 from the rear galley to the cockpit door is 110 feet. The aisle was narrow, with only enough room for them to move in single file from the rear of the plane to the cockpit. Within a very short span of time, the courageous passengers charged the cockpit. Such fortitude!

I wish Norman Rockwell could have been there to paint a canvas record of "America in Progress."

From 9:58 A.M. to 10:06 A.M. the cockpit voice recorder picked up sounds of a death struggle: a crash of dishes and trays being hurled; the voices of the hijackers calling to each other to "hold the door!" One of the passengers cried, "Let's get them!" Whether the hijackers were fighting amongst themselves or the passengers had gotten through the cockpit and were trying to take over, we cannot be sure. A man's voice was heard to say, "Give it to me!"

Mark it down, and get ready to shout! At that moment, it was not the passengers but the terrorists who were afraid!

In the midst of the struggle, the cowardly lunatic at the cockpit controls lowered the nose, putting the aircraft into a steep and irreversible dive.

At 10:06 A.M. Flight 93 crashed into a Pennsylvania field. I've seen the list of the debris that was retrieved, including one seat many, many yards from that fifty-foot crater; a tied necktie; a Bible with just a little bit of the cover dog-eared, the rest of it in excellent condition.

It wasn't marked on the recovery list, but I would say that they also found the spirit of America. What makes our nation great is not the skyscrapers, the financial success or the size of our estates. It is the spirit that causes ordinary men to rise up against tyranny, the spirit that demands an unrestrained freedom to worship and serve God, the spirit that pays willingly the price of freedom.

If that plane, Flight 93, had remained on its altered course under the command of those murderous madmen, in just twenty more minutes it would have been over the U.S. Capitol or the White House. Subsequent data indicate it was probably targeted at the White House.

Dr. Clyde Box poetically described this great feat of fortitude and fearlessness:

> **"Let's roll!" The cry resounded through the plane**
> **Where men and women sat in fear,**
> **Knowing not what the future held—**
> **Perhaps cruel death was inching near.**
>
> **They called their loved ones on the phone**
> **to tell them of their plight.**

Terrorists had taken over the plane;
    This well could be their final flight.

They proclaimed their love to their wives;
    They knew what lay ahead.
Though what they did could save some lives,
    Their deed could leave them dead.

Without hesitation and without regret,
    Knowing their action would take its toll,
One of the brave ones rose to his feet
    And shouted to the others, "Let's roll!"

If those gallant passengers could rally together as they did on 9/11, then certainly the God-fearing, Bible-believing, born-again Christians in our fundamental churches can rally together and fight the forces of Hell by uniting in our soul-winning efforts to win more people to Christ.

Fortitude matters.

When I think about our American heroes, it makes me want to say the Pledge of Allegiance and sing the "Star-Spangled Banner."

Our salvation is in our precious Saviour, not the president of the United States. But when President Bush spoke live to the public, we could see that he was moved with emotion. My wife and I stood together and openly wept; and when he finished his speech, I said to my son, "If I were a little bit younger, I'd sign up!"

I believe God in Heaven providentially has put George W. Bush at the helm of this nation for such a time as this. I shudder to think what this nation would be like and how different this day might have been if a skirt chaser were still in the White House.

At the Flight 93 crash site, I believe we see the fingerprint of God. He is saying to us on this anniversary of that awful tragedy, "Faith matters, family matters and fortitude matters!"

I hope America is pondering these powerful truths from Flight 93.

Chapter 7

ROADBLOCKS ON THE
ROAD TO REVIVAL

"Your iniquities have turned away these things, and your sins have withholden good things from you."—Jer. 5:25.

When revival does not come, there is a reason! When you are not fervent for God, there is a reason! When you are not winning souls, there is a reason! In a word, the reason is sin! It is necessary for us to understand that sin is like oil that will not mix with the water of a spiritual awakening. Sin and a spiritual awakening are at opposite ends of the spectrum. They are always at odds with each other!

It is impossible for believers and Bible-believing churches to experience a mighty move of God, a real Heaven-sent revival, as long as sin is being enjoyed.

Jeremiah, the weeping prophet, dealt specifically with the backslidden nation of Israel (Jeremiah 5). He denounced four different sins that they were openly committing: (1) perverseness (vss. 1–6); (2) adultery (vss. 7–9); (3) impiety (vss. 10–17); and (4) spiritual and civil corruption (vss. 18–31).

It is good that Jeremiah, the preacher of God, under the direct inspiration of the Holy Spirit, confronts their spiritual and civil corruption. He says, "Your iniquities have turned away these things, and your sins have withholden good things from you."

The word "withholden" in the Hebrew language means "to deny, to keep or to refrain." In this great verse on revival, we see that turning from sin is absolutely necessary if we expect to have a true and triumphant revival.

There is more to having a meeting than just inviting an evangelist. There is more to having a meeting than just passing out a sharp-looking flier. There is more to having a meeting than just setting aside several days for services. If we are going to have a spiritual awakening, a revival—a time when God meets with us and we meet with God—then it is necessary that you and I turn from known sin. In the great, classic Old Testament verse on revival, the Bible says, "If my people, which are called by my name, shall humble themselves, and pray, and seek my face, and turn from their wicked ways; then will I hear from heaven, and will forgive their sin, and will heal their land" (II Chron. 7:14).

You and I are fooling ourselves if we think we will have revival before we have turned away from our sins. It is sin that stands in the way of a mighty move of God.

If I were to ask each of you what sin keeps back the blessings of revival, what sin hinders revival in your church, possibly no two people would name the same sin; and there would be no wrong answers, because every sin named would be a sin to keep God from sending a revival.

If someone said, "The sin of not praying keeps a Christian and the church from having revival," I'd say, "Amen!" If someone said, "The sin of gossip keeps the Christian and the church from having revival," I'd say,

"Amen!" If someone said, "The sin of not soul winning keeps the Christian and the church from revival," I'd say, "Amen!"

There are, however, three specific sins which are committed perhaps more than any others by God's people. Each one stands as a dam before the reservoir of a spiritual awakening. They are indeed "roadblocks on the road to revival."

I. THE SIN OF UNFORGIVENESS

"And if he trespass against thee seven times in a day, and seven times in a day turn again to thee, saying, I repent; thou shalt forgive him."—Luke 17:4.

The Lord Jesus Christ told His disciples that they were to forgive those who had wronged them. He explained to them that if someone offended them seven times in a twenty-four-hour period and yet asked for pardon seven times, he should be completely forgiven seven times!

Unforgiveness can stand in the way of a spiritual awakening. There are many believers who sit in the pews of fundamental churches who have been lied about, mistreated and falsely accused. As a result, they refuse to forgive the persons who offended them.

People who have suffered false accusations, mistreatment and lies have often said to me, "You just don't understand. I've not been treated right."

Whenever I hear that, I think how laughable it is! I came into the world mistreated. I wasn't outside the womb five minutes before a complete stranger held me by one leg, hung me upside down and slapped me on my backside—and for no apparent reason! It hurt, and I cried, but I've gotten over it.

A lot of God's people, in fact some of us, need to get over

being lied about and mistreated and falsely accused. Recently someone said to me, "Oh, Preacher, people are saying terrible things about me." I looked at him and said, "Praise the Lord!" He said, "Why would you praise the Lord?" I said, "Because if they're talking about you, that means they're not talking about me right now. So praise the Lord!"

Being talked about is just part of life. It is a predictable part of the Christian walk. It's just what happens when you serve God. Nonetheless, I am afraid some dear Christian has unforgiveness in his heart, and that's the reason that we do not now have revival.

Mark it down! The wrong they committed against you does not entitle you to do the wrong you are now committing against them. That's right! They may never do you right, but you should cleanse your heart with forgiveness. Hold no grudge. Give yourself with a clean heart to the Lord.

It's abundantly clear! If we want to experience revival, you and I need to deal with the sin of unforgiveness.

The Bible says, "And be ye kind one to another, tenderhearted, forgiving one another, even as God for Christ's sake hath forgiven you" (Eph. 4:32).

As a believer you should always forgive those who hurt you, and here's why:

1. It keeps you, the believer, on praying ground. "If I regard iniquity in my heart, the Lord will not hear me" (Ps. 66:18).

You forfeit your prayer power when you fail to forgive people who have somehow harmed you.

I pray about many important things every single day of the world. I pray about my precious family—my wife, my son and my daughter. I pray about my vital ministry, and I'm not saying it's vital because it is *my* ministry. Every preacher would agree that his ministry is vital. I pray about my intimate walk with the Lord. I pray about a lot of important things.

I simply cannot afford to forfeit the ear of God when I pray by having unforgiveness in my heart toward someone else. There are many things of too great significance that I pray about in the course of the day.

Don't you have much to pray about too? Surely you do! If you'll keep forgiving, it will keep you on praying ground.

2. It is Christlike. "Then said Jesus, Father, forgive them; for they know not what they do" (Luke 23:34).

The believer should also forgive those who have hurt him because it is Christlike to do so. If Jesus could pardon those who so seriously and horribly mistreated Him, then you can gladly pardon those who have only slightly mistreated you.

You take that mistreatment that has come your way and put it alongside Calvary. See how quickly it pales in comparison. What you and I have gone through isn't even close to what Jesus went through so that we might be saved. When we forgive, it is Christlike.

3. It wards off bitterness. "Looking diligently lest any man fail of the grace of God; lest any root of bitterness springing up trouble you, and thereby many be defiled" (Heb. 12:15).

The believer should always—and "always" is a key word— forgive those who hurt him, because it wards off bitterness. You never have to worry about a root of bitterness if you'll keep the soil of your heart plowed over with forgiveness.

73

Here's the staggering truth about bitterness: It not only affects you, but it also affects everyone with whom you come in contact. Your bitterness will contaminate others if you give it place.

You're not listening here to someone who rode in late this afternoon on the back end of a truckload of pumpkins. I didn't just start preaching yesterday. I've seen it happen many times. I have watched a Christian get a burr under his blanket. Soon he is not the only one that is disgruntled. First it's the husband, but soon it's the husband and the wife who are disgruntled. Before long, the children are disgruntled as well.

There is no more serious disease than a spiritual cancer—a bitterness that will spread through your heart and out into your home and then throughout your church family. You've got to stop it before it starts! Don't let it happen!

The believer should always forgive those who hurt him so that the seeds of bitterness will be swept away. Oh, that every single blood-bought believer would realize that he should forgive and forgive and forgive and forgive yet again!

Yes, it is great when we understand that forgiveness will keep one on praying ground! It is Christlike, and it wards off bitterness!

Last year I was in New England for a revival meeting. On Sunday night I preached along the same subject that I'm now addressing. I gave the invitation, the Lord met with us, and there were many people kneeling from one end of the altar to the other. It was glorious to see the people doing business with God at His altar.

When the service was over, an elderly lady came to me,

weeping uncontrollably, and she said to me, "Preacher, thank you! Thank you for preaching on what you preached on tonight, because I got right with the Lord and right with another lady in this church with whom I've not spoken for three long years."

She went on to explain that for three full years—that's 1,095 days—they hadn't spoken a word to each other, even though they were members of the same church. That means they were washed in the same blood by the same Spirit and believed the very same Book, but they hadn't spoken to each other for 156 weeks, three solid years—not even a "hello" or a "good-bye."

She told me that if she and the other woman were both coming in the same door, one would turn and find another door. If they both started walking down the same aisle, one would turn and go down another aisle. They could not even talk to the same people at the same time. This went on for thirty-six months, three agonizingly long years.

Then she said, "I went to that lady tonight and said, 'I owe you an apology,' but the other lady said quickly, 'No, I owe you an apology.'" They almost got into a fight over whose fault it was, but then they both got right with God and with each other!

The next night that same sister in the faith came up to me before the service, hugged my neck and said, "The joy bells are ringing again, and I'm enjoying my Christian life as I haven't enjoyed it for three long years."

I'm thankful that I can enter any door I want to use. I'm thankful that I can walk down any aisle I want to use. I'm thankful that I can talk to any person with whom I want to talk.

That's the way it ought to be with all of us in the house of God.

If you are watching doors, checking aisles and spying on people to see who is and who isn't there, you need to do something about it right now. Take care of it by building an altar and putting your unforgiving spirit under the blood.

Let me say this about the altar: it is the place to do business with God. There is no Christian, no matter how long he has been saved or what position he holds in the church, that gets past using an old-fashioned altar. When God speaks to your heart, it shouldn't take fifteen verses of "Just As I Am" to get you moving. Brother, you ought to hit the altar speedily and do business with God.

If you have a problem with someone, don't try to figure out whose fault it is—just get it under the blood. Apologize whether or not it's your fault, and then go on for God together.

God knows that I'm not trying to be harsh, but sometimes I get in a meeting and feel as if I want to draw maps to the altar, have them copied and pass them out each night during the services. So many Christian people don't have a clue as to where the altar is. They can't seem ever to find their way to it!

The sin of unforgiveness will keep God from sending a revival!

II. THE SIN OF UNBELIEF

"And he did not many mighty works there because of their unbelief."—Matt. 13:58.

The Lord Jesus Christ did not do a large number of supernatural things in the town of Nazareth because of the people's disbelief in Him.

Evangelist Oliver B. Greene said, "Unbelief is the ugliest sin that a moral man can commit against Almighty God!"

Unbelief stands tall in the way of the advance of a spiritual awakening.

Many believers who sit in fundamental church pews today feel that you can no longer build a great church, that their lost ones are not going to be saved, and that the days of sweeping revivals are over. Oh, what tragic unbelief! What colossal spiritual failure that is!

Friend, you and I need to deal with the sin of unbelief!

The Bible says, "For with God nothing shall be impossible" (Luke 1:37). I love that word "nothing." It is a compound word! Nothing is really "no thing"! Oh, if believers would ask God to write that verse upon their hearts, they would happily believe that their church will grow, that their lost loved ones will be saved, and that they will be part of a sweeping revival.

People can be saved and added to the church. Families can still be reached for God! The Gospel still works!

Listen, if there is one funeral that we need to preach in our fundamental churches, it is the funeral of unbelief.

These days it seems like the work of God is overrun with disbelief. People say, "It cannot be done! It will not work! It will never happen!"

Dr. Curtis Hutson said, "Those who say it can't be done are those who have never done it in any age or dispensation." It *can* be done!

Last week I was in a revival meeting in Ohio, and God was so good to us. We had seventeen people saved, and five of them were senior citizens—the youngest was seventy; the oldest, eighty-three! Five senior citizens saved in one revival meeting. Wonderful it was!

During that meeting another elderly lady came to me (she had been to three meetings in a row), and she said, "Now, I have a boyfriend who wants my hand in marriage, but I won't give it to him because he is not saved. He goes to an Episcopalian church. He doesn't want anyone—even the pastor—to talk to him about God. Men from the church have gone to him, and he turns them away. He'll be in at least one of the meetings here this week, but you can forget about him getting saved."

I said, "Let's just have him come and see what God is going to do."

She said, "Well, all right, but he's not going to get saved. I'm not going to marry him, and I'm not going to tell him that if he gets saved I will marry him, because then he might make a false profession. I know he's not going to get saved, and I know I'm not going to marry him!"

On Sunday morning this man went to his Episcopalian church, and then Sunday night he came to our meeting. Now understand, if you take an Episcopalian church, any Episcopalian church, and compare it to a fundamental, soul-winning Baptist church where people are on fire for God and happy about serving God, you'll see that the two groups are poles apart. So when he came on Sunday night, he acted like he was in shock. Honestly, he'd never heard anything like our Baptist church before.

After the service the lady said to me, "He came tonight, but he's not coming back, especially the way you preached.

There is no way he's coming back."

But guess what. The next night he was there, and about halfway through the service I thought he started to act like he was enjoying what was going on. The next night he came back. This was three nights straight! Oh, God was working with him and dealing with him, but he didn't come back the next night. My heart sank.

We extended the meeting one more night, and he came back once again. After the Bible was read and preached and the invitation given, this man of seventy-six years stepped out, walked down that aisle, knelt at the altar and was promptly born into the family of God.

When that dear sister saw him at the altar, she began to shout. She came to the altar and knelt right beside him. She rejoiced in his coming to Christ. After the service, she came to me and said, "You were right! I should have known that God is still able and that we can still see people saved!"

I'm so glad God is still in the soul-saving business. I'm glad that God can still take people from the darkness of sin to meet the Light of the world, the Lord Jesus Christ. I'm glad we can still have revival!

It doesn't matter if someone is seventy-six years old and going to an Episcopalian church, God is still in the soul-saving business. He is still in the church-building business. God is still able to give revival to his people. But where the sin of unbelief holds sway, we just don't see it happen.

When the famous missionary Hudson Taylor first went to China, it was in a sailing vessel. Very close to the shore of some islands where cannibals lived, the ship was becalmed, and it slowly drifted toward the shore, unable to go forward.

The savages were gathering, anticipating a feast.

The captain said to Mr. Taylor, "You need to pray for the help of God." Hudson Taylor said, "I will do so only if you will hoist the sails to catch the breeze." The captain said, "No, you just need to pray. When the wind comes, then I'll set the sails." Hudson Taylor said, "No! I'm not going to pray until you set the sails to catch the wind." The captain said, "I'm not going to do it."

Hudson Taylor went to his stateroom, and the ship drifted closer and closer to that island of cannibals. It seemed like the closer they got to the shore, the more cannibals appeared. Wouldn't you know it! The captain had a change of heart.

He came to Mr. Taylor's stateroom, and he said, "All right, I'll set the sail. You pray!"

The sails were raised, and Hudson Taylor went on his face before God. In only a few minutes there came another knock on his stateroom door. The captain said, "Are you still praying?" He said, "Yes, I am." The captain said, "Then please stop because we have more wind than we know what to do with!"

Listen, Christian! God is never going to move the vessel of our lives until by faith we raise the sails!

The sin of unbelief will keep God from sending a revival!

III. THE SIN OF UNCONCERN

"Brethren, my heart's desire and prayer to God for Israel is, that they might be saved."—Rom. 10:1.

The apostle Paul had a consuming passion to see his

nation, Israel, brought to a saving knowledge of the Lord Jesus Christ.

Unconcern is one of the major sticking points that stands in the way of a spiritual awakening. Many believers who sit in fundamental church pews never tell a single soul about Jesus. They don't even pass out gospel tracts. They don't go to the altar to pray for the unsaved people that they know.

You and I need to deal with the sin of unconcern.

The Bibles says, "Awake to righteousness, and sin not; for some have not the knowledge of God: I speak this to your shame" (I Cor. 15:34).

When a believer does not care where a lost soul is going to spend eternity, that believer—regardless of what visible position he may hold in the church—has laid his head on the pillow of complacency and has covered himself with the blanket of indifference.

You may be a member of a great soul-winning church and the testimony of that church may be a national testimony and people all across this country may know it is a church where soul winning is supreme, but you may still be a member of that church and not be the least interested in souls. You can be a member of that church and never tell anyone about Jesus. You can be a member of that church and never pass out a gospel tract.

I am almost to the place where I feel like I am not fully clothed if I don't have gospel tracts on my person.

You can be a member of a great soul-winning church and yet never go to the altar and pray for people you know who are lost.

The sin of unconcern in you will keep God from sending

a revival! When we are not bothered by the fact that people are dying all around us and going to a literal Hell, when it just doesn't affect us one way or the other, the awful truth is that we just don't care!

We think because we have a soul-winning church, because we have a great printing ministry or because our pastor is an effective soul winner, it's just not for us. It's that awful attitude, dear friend, that keeps revival from us.

Evangelist Gipsy Smith, a man used of God in a mighty way, often told about the conversion of his Uncle Rodney. Among Gypsies it was not considered proper for a child to address his elders unless spoken to. This would be doubly true if a child spoke to an elder about spiritual matters.

Young Gipsy Smith had a burden for his uncle, and he prayed and waited for his opportunity to talk with him. One day, Uncle Rodney said to his nephew, "Lad, how is it that your suit is new but the trousers are nearly worn through at the knees?" Gipsy looked at his uncle and said, "I've worn the knees through praying for you, Uncle Rodney, and I want so much for God to make you a Christian."

Gipsy Smith told how his Uncle Rodney put his arms around him in a fatherly embrace, then fell to his knees and right then and there received Christ as his Saviour.

Don't you think that the Uncle Rodneys we know would come to Christ a whole lot quicker if we had the burden that Gipsy Smith had for his uncle? The sin of unconcern is a pathetic matter, isn't it?

So here they are—three sins that keep God from sending revival. There are other sins that keep us from having revival—the sin of not praying, the sin of gossip, the sin of moral failure—but the three big sins, I believe the main ones, are the sin of unforgiveness, the sin of unbelief and the sin of unconcern. These sins will keep revival dammed up and never able to break loose. As a great wall, they are major impediments to what God wants to do for us.

The Gospel is the death, the burial and the resurrection of the Lord Jesus Christ (I Cor. 15:1-4). He died for you; He was buried for you; He rose again from the dead that you might be saved.

> **Jesus paid it all;**
> **All to him I owe.**
> **Sin had left a crimson stain;**
> **He washed it white as snow.**

I pray that not one of you would grieve the Holy Spirit or resist the Holy Spirit or quench the Holy Spirit! May this be a great time of great victory. Let's not delay! Let's not give place to those "roadblocks on the road to revival." Let's have revival!

Chapter 8

WHATEVER HAPPENED
TO HELL?

"For a fire is kindled in mine anger, and shall burn unto the lowest hell, and shall consume the earth with her increase, and set on fire the foundations of the mountains."—Deut. 32:22.

In this verse there is a four-letter word that is so awesome and so awful, it is almost unspeakable. It is the word "hell."

The same holy volume that tells us about a place where there are gates of pearl also tells us about a place where there is gnashing of teeth. The word "hell" in Hebrew means "the world of the dead."

Between the covers of the Bible, the word is so explained as to describe that residential region in the world beyond life where the unsaved masses are incarcerated for eternity.

In Deuteronomy 32 we have the final song of the prophet Moses. The song reveals God's greatness in the context of His historical dealings with the nation of Israel. So important was it that this song be heard that Moses did not hesitate to call for Heaven's and earth's ears: "Give ear, O ye heavens, and I will speak; and hear, O earth, the words of my mouth" (vs. 1).

Does it not seem noteworthy to you that this song

addressed to both the eternal world and the temporal world had a stanza in it dealing with a literal Hell. "For a fire is kindled in mine anger, and shall burn unto the lowest hell, and shall consume the earth with her increase, and set on fire the foundations of the mountains" (vs. 22).

This is the first of fifty-four times that the word "hell" is found in the Word of God. If you miss everything else I say, I pray that you not miss this fact: The Hell of the Bible is the Hell of eternity. It is a real place, a literal place, and a place to which you do not want to go.

Notice these three things the Bible clearly teaches concerning Hell.

I. HELL IS A HOT PLACE

"[His angels] *shall cast them into a furnace of fire: there shall be wailing and gnashing of teeth.*"—Matt. 13:42.

The Bible says that Hell, "a furnace of fire," is a hot place. When the unsaved cross the great divide from life into eternity, they will experience terrific heat.

You may be asking yourselves: *How could a body be engulfed in the flames and not be entirely consumed?* I'll give you the answer. Once God made a bush burn, and it was not consumed, so certainly God can make a body burn without consuming it.

"And the angel of the LORD appeared unto him in a flame of fire out of the midst of a bush: and he looked, and, behold, the bush burned with fire, and the bush was not consumed."— Exod. 3:2.

I read where a world-renowned evangelist said in *Time* magazine (November 15, 1993 issue): "When it comes to a literal fire, I don't preach it, because I'm not sure about it." That fellow either needs to buy a Bible or blow the dust off the one he already has, because you can't miss it in the Bible—Hell is a hot place!

You shouldn't give ear to anyone who tries to air-condition Hell. If someone is trying to do that, then they must be making plans to move in.

There are three things that prove that Hell is a hot place:

1. It's proven by the testimony of the Saviour. "I say unto you… whosoever shall say to his brother, Raca, shall be in danger of the council: but whosoever shall say, Thou fool, shall be in danger of hell fire." (Matt. 5:22).

We know that Hell is an inferno because of the testimony of the Saviour. The Lord Jesus Christ was a fire-and-brimstone Preacher! He preached more about a literal Hell than He ever preached about Heaven.

People come to me and say, "Preacher, you are a fire-and-brimstone preacher." I don't know if they mean that as a compliment or a criticism, but I take it as a compliment, because it puts me in the good company of Jesus.

2. It's proven by two sinful cities. "Even as Sodom and Gomorrha, and the cities about them in like manner, giving themselves over to fornication, and going after strange flesh, are set forth for an example, suffering the vengeance of eternal fire" (Jude 7).

These two sinful cities are another proof that Hell is real. The judged metropolises of Sodom and Gomorrha give us stirring illustrations that there is fire in Hell.

3. It's proven by the tears of the sinner. "And he cried and said, Father Abraham, have mercy on me, and send

Lazarus, that he may dip the tip of his finger in water, and cool my tongue; for I am tormented in this flame" (Luke 16:24).

The tears of the sinner are another proof that there are flames in Hell. One of the things that caused the rich man to weep in eternity was the extreme heat.

For well over two hundred years, a fire that was started with the use of flint and steel by Tom Dalton in his Blue Ridge Mountain cabin has been kept burning. The fire has been moved from one cabin to another as the old ones have given place to the newer ones. Generation after generation of Dalton's descendants have watched it carefully through the years. Today it is the oldest fire in the United States, perhaps the world. It has been no easy task, because even in hot weather, it requires a cord of wood per month, but the fire has always burned on.

But wait a minute. There is another fire that has burned longer than Tom Dalton's fire, and that is the flames of Hell, a hot place.

II. HELL IS A HORRIBLE PLACE

"The wicked shall be turned into hell, and all the nations that forget God."—Ps. 9:17.

Yes, Hell is a horrible place. The Bible says so! When the unsaved enter eternity, they will be entering into a godless, wicked society surrounded by the most extreme and terrible people who ever lived.

The word "wicked" in Hebrew means "morally wrong." Try to imagine what it would be like to spend just one hour with Jack the Ripper, Adolph Hitler or Jeffrey Dahmer. That would be a horrifying sixty minutes, but the sinner will be sentenced to spend forever with those types of sinfully depraved people.

Listen, I wouldn't want to have to spend even one minute, let alone an hour, with Jack the Ripper or Hitler or Dahmer; but these are the types of people you will spend eternity with if you are lost—the scum of society.

When I've been witnessing, I've heard people say, "Oh, when I go to Hell, it's going to be a beer bash. When I go to Hell, it's going to be a card party. When I go to Hell, it's going to be a great thing." Listen! You can't find even one verse—or a portion of a verse—in the Bible that suggests that there will be a good time at any time in Hell. You can find a truckload of verses that say the opposite.

Friend, you and I must come to see Hell as the Bible says Hell is. Hell is a tragically horrible place.

When God gives the roll call of Hell, He mentions eight different types of people who will be there: "But the fearful, and unbelieving, and the abominable, and murderers, and whoremongers, and sorcerers, and idolaters, and all liars, shall have their part in the lake which burneth with fire and brimstone: which is the second death"—Rev. 21:8.

Everyone now in Hell, as well as those who will one day be in Hell, can be placed in one of those eight classes of people.

First, there are the fearful. The fearful are the people who are afraid to confess the Lord Jesus Christ. I believe that our churches are filled with the fearful. They come Sunday morning, and they come Sunday night. Some come at the midweek service to the house of God, all the while knowing in their heart of hearts that they are not saved.

They're afraid to be saved. They're afraid of what someone might say or think. Let me assure you that anyone who is saved and right with God will say a good word and think a good thing about you when you come to be saved.

Second, there are the unbelieving. The unbelieving are people who are in possession of the truth but are unwilling to trust the Lord Jesus Christ.

There are also the abominable. The abominable are the ones who are given over to various indulgences of immorality.

Next, there are the murderers. They are the hideous fiends who have no respect for life. They are the savage killers.

Fifth, in Hell will be the whoremongers. This speaks of those who are driven by lust and practice fornication.

Then there are the sorcerers. Sorcerers are people who work with evil spirits. You'll find them saying, "Call my 900 number, and I'll predict your future." If you call them, they'll ask, "Who's calling?" Aren't they supposed to know that already.

A seventh class will be the idolaters. The idolaters insult God by worshiping images.

Eighth, there are the liars. They are compulsive deceivers; they have no love for or loyalty to the truth.

Just one of these eight groups of people would cause any sensible person to be saved so he would not have to spend eternity with them!

A certain young lady went home for the summer after graduating from college. Her parents had prayed that she might be saved, and for the first week she was home, her parents took her with them to a revival campaign.

Throughout the meeting the Holy Ghost convicted her mightily, but she would not trust the Lord Jesus Christ.

Following the revival, she was making a trip with her father on a train. Her father stepped out of the car for a moment, and when he came back, he found his daughter in tears.

She said, "Daddy, let's get out of here. Let's go into the smoker."

He said, "No, darling, it's filled with smoke and men. You don't want to go there."

She said, "O Daddy, we must get out of here." She ran out of that car and into the smoking car. Her father followed her, and he lowered the window in the car to let in some fresh air.

She said, "O Daddy, while you were gone, the men back in the other car used vulgar language, and it shocked my modesty. They are such terrible men." Then she dropped her head on her father's shoulder and began to cry.

Her father wisely looked at her and said, "Darling, unless you get saved, that is the same kind of people with whom you are going to spend the ceaseless ages of eternity in Hell!"

She said, "O Daddy, I want to be saved!" Right then and there in the smoking car, she bowed her head, humbled her heart and was born into the family of God!

III. HELL IS A HOLDING PLACE

"And death and hell were cast into the lake of fire. This is the second death."—Rev. 20:14.

The Bible clearly teaches that Hell is a hot place and a horrible place and a holding place.

When the unsaved enter eternity, they will go to a place of temporary confinement. Some of you are thinking, *Well, I've never heard that before.* Then listen closely.

Evangelist Oliver B. Greene once wrote this about Revelation 20:14:

> Hell is located in the center of this earth. It is a prison to hold wicked sinners [and I add, the unsaved] until the consummation of all things and the beginning of the eternity of eternities. At that time, Hell itself will be cast into the lake of fire, which is the eternal abode of wicked spirits [I add again, the unsaved].

Friend, you and I must comprehend that Hell is a holding place.

The Bible says, "Therefore hell hath enlarged herself, and opened her mouth without measure" (Isa. 5:14). Mark it down, Hell will enlarge itself until after the great white throne judgment, when it will be cast into the lake of fire.

When people are lost and die without Christ, they immediately go to Hell! There'll be a day when all those who are in Hell will be delivered to stand before the great white throne judgment, and from there they'll be sent to the lake of fire!

It is my conviction that, as serious as Hell is, the lake of fire is even more serious, because Hell is going to be taken and cast into the lake of fire.

Harry Houdini was known as the man who could get out of anything. He was a world-famous escape artist. Many times he would free himself from handcuffs, mailbags and straitjackets. I've seen some rare film footage of Houdini covered with shackles and manacles and handcuffs, and it seemed like in no time at all he freed himself from those devices of bondage. Houdini could seemingly get out of anything.

On January 6, 1906, he went to the United States federal jail in Washington, D.C., and challenged the warden to lock him in a cell and let him try to escape. The warden agreed to his request.

Houdini was stripped of his clothing and locked in the south wing in the middle chamber of three heavily barred cubbyholes which were walled in solid masonry. His clothes were locked in another of the three cells. In twenty-one minutes, Houdini was fully clothed and standing in the warden's office. He had escaped from a federal prison!

Houdini may have been able to get out of man's prison house, but no one, not even Houdini himself, will be able to escape from God's prison house. Once you are there, you are there forever!

Hell is a holding place, but thank God there is good news! Jesus left Heaven and came to this world filled with sin and sorrow. He lived a sinless life in total obedience to God's law. He then fulfilled many Scriptures by His cruel death on the cross and His supernatural resurrection from the dead so that you might be saved.

You need to receive Jesus today. I'm not talking about church membership. Redemption is a free gift to all who will just receive Him. Leave the darkness of the world and find the Light and become a child of God. Not only will you avoid going to Hell, you'll go to Heaven!

I believe any time a preacher preaches on this subject, Christians think about people they know who are unsaved.

How can Christians hear a preacher preach on Hell and not get a new, fresh, greater desire to see family and friends and fellow workers brought to the Lord Jesus Christ?

Hell is a hot place, a horrible place and a holding place. Thinking about Hell ought to make an unsaved person get saved. Thinking about Hell ought to make a saved person become a soul winner. It ought to make us ask for a greater vision, a greater burden, a greater desire in seeing the lost saved, because the lost are just one heartbeat away from Hell.

You don't have to go to Hell—Jesus died for you; He was buried for you; He arose again from the dead for you. I wish my vocabulary were better, because I don't even come close to being able to express the awfulness of Hell. If God has spoken to your heart about your need to be saved, come to Him now.

Christian, God bless that preacher that preached to you and brought you to faith in Christ. God bless that soul winner that came to your house and led you to the Lord. God bless that person who prayed for you, whose prayers brought you to the foot of the cross. God bless those who had a burden for your soul. The burden that they had for you is the burden that you need for others.

I pray that God will bless His Word to meet your particular need.

Editor's Invitation to Come to Christ

Dear friend, you have read the Bible's description of Hell. As there is an eternal Heaven of bliss for those who receive Christ as Saviour, so there must be an eternal Hell of misery for those who reject Him until they die.

There is not one sane reason for wanting to go to Hell, and the good news is that no one has to! The death of Jesus on the cross was His payment for your sins so that God could pardon you without violating His own holy nature. The resurrection of Jesus from the grave was testimony that He had conquered death and that as a living Saviour He could give us eternal life with Him. His resurrection was also God's guarantee that He had accepted that payment for all who will by faith come to Jesus and trust His payment to reconcile them to God.

Will you now simply ask Christ to save your soul from an endless Hell? He said, "Him that cometh to me I will in no wise cast out" (John 6:37). God promised: "As many as received him [Jesus], to them gave he power to become the sons of God" (John 1:12). If you make a decision today to trust Jesus alone to bring you to God and take you to Heaven when you die, would you write me a letter to let me know of your decision? The address is Dr. Shelton Smith, P.O. Box 1099, Murfreesboro, Tennessee 37133. I would like to send you some free literature that will help you in your new life for Christ.

Chapter 9

LIGHTS OUT AT THE CHURCH HOUSE!

"And the child Samuel ministered unto the LORD before Eli. And the word of the LORD was precious in those days; there was no open vision.

"And it came to pass at that time, when Eli was laid down in his place, and his eyes began to wax dim, that he could not see;

"And ere the lamp of God went out in the temple of the LORD, where the ark of God was, and Samuel was laid down to sleep."—I Sam. 3:1–3.

There is no sadder news than the announcement that a church has lost its spiritual illumination.

As unthinkable as it is, the tragic truth is that the lamp of God is almost extinguished in the house of God. "Ere the lamp of God went out in the temple of the LORD" (vs. 3).

The lamp of God is also referred to in Scripture as the "candlestick of pure gold," with three branches on each side, thus affording room for seven lamps which were supplied with olive oil. The candlestick stood on the south side of the Holy Place, and its snuffers and tongs were made of pure gold (Exod. 25:31–38; 26:35).

This, the lamp of God, is a type of spiritual illumination and occupation. The moment that a church loses its light, it has lost any and all sense of heavenly perception and visitation. So in this message we will raise the alert level to make us aware of this impending tragedy.

We can lose our natural illumination and still be in business, but if we lose that supernatural illumination, we may as well hang a sign on the door that says, "Out of Business."

All across our country there are churches that were at one time lighthouses for the Lord, but they've lost their light, and they are no longer in business for God. They may still have services, but spiritually the light is out. They are grasping in the shadows and stumbling through the darkness.

Any church can lose its light, and once it's gone, God can't bless it, use it or benefit it as a church. As much as He wants to do it, He cannot.

Three things invariably happen that cause the light to go out in the house of God.

I. THE LIGHT GOES OUT WHEN NO BIBLE IS PROCLAIMED

"Peter, standing up with the eleven, lifted up his voice, and said unto them, Ye men of Judæa, and all ye that dwell at Jerusalem, be this known unto you, and hearken to my words."—Acts 2:14.

On the day of Pentecost the apostle Peter stood up and in a forceful, firm and fiery way declared the Word of God.

The way we conduct our church services should not be by man's whim, but by God's will. We clearly see in this verse the New Testament model for conducting present-day church services.

Too many of our churches are going in the wrong direction today. When it comes to building up the work of God, they take a neighborhood survey to find out what people want or don't want, then they add to or delete from the service to accommodate the wishes of the people. The community surrounding the church should not be setting the pace. The church, anchored in the authority of God's Word, should set the pace. Furthermore, the people in the pew inside the church should not be setting the pace either. The pastor, who is the man of God, should be setting the pace.

A majority of churches today have no Bibles, no hymnbooks, no invitations, no baptistries, no man of God in the pulpit, no ecclesiastical separation and no personal separation from the world.

In some cities it's difficult to tell the local church from the public library! Inside they explain the things of the world and how to overcome them, but the things of God are not expounded at all.

On the day of Pentecost (Acts 2) there was a gathering—a group of believers and the disciples. Peter, God's mouthpiece, expounded excitedly God's Word (Joel 2:28–32); and they had great results: 3,000 people were saved.

If God worked so mightily in the past, He will work mightily in the present! But, you mark it down, the light will go out in the house of God when there is no Bible proclaimed.

"Preach the word; be instant in season, out of season; reprove, rebuke, exhort with all longsuffering and doctrine."—II Tim. 4:2.

From coast to coast in our country, some academics and the church-growth gurus are coaching men of God to be "calm communicators," "sharers of relevant information," and never to come across as dogmatic in their delivery.

When a preacher mounts the pulpit, he shouldn't sound like a mossed-over newsman reading the hog market reports on the noon news. A preacher shouldn't **share** information; **sharing** is what you do in kindergarten with cookies and crayons. A man of God is to be a man of God!

God has given every preacher a delivery, a style and a way of preaching that is distinctive to his own personality. No two preachers should look alike, sound alike or preach in the same fashion, because God made every one of us different from everyone else. Each one of us is as unique in design as a snowflake or a fingerprint. But when we preach, we should all have urgency, fire and punch in our sermons.

Someone said to me, "If I preached like you, I'd make people mad."

I said, "It's not *how* you preach that makes people mad; it's *what* you preach that makes them mad!"

If the world can get excited about the temporal, then the man of God should get excited about the eternal.

Some time ago a lady came up to me at a meeting and said to me, "It's not right!"

"What?"

"I can't believe it!"

"What?"

"It's not fair!"

"What?"

"I saw a boxer fight the other night, and I believe he has stolen all of your moves!"

I couldn't think of an answer to that!

At another meeting a teenager came up to me and said, "I want you to know that all that bobbing and bouncing around you do when you preach makes me seasick."

The next night her father said, "Preacher, I've got good news for you. My entire family will enjoy your preaching tonight because on my way here I stopped at the pharmacy and bought motion-sickness pills!"

I couldn't think of an answer to that either!

A person can take the English alphabet and the eternal Word of God and describe clearly what their position is on what scriptural preaching ought to be. Here we go. The Bible says that preaching is

Anointed (Isa. 61:1)

Befitting in a palace or a poorhouse (I Kings 17:1)

Commanded (Mark 16:15)

Demanding of a decision (Acts 3:19)

Essential (Rom. 10:14)

Fundamental (II Tim. 4:2)

Gratifying (Acts 16:33)

Hot (Heb. 1:7)

Imperative (I Cor. 9:16)

Just what the world and the church need (I Cor. 1:17)

Kingly (Matt. 2:2)

Lengthy and lovely (Acts 20:9; Rom. 10:15)

Magnetic (Matt. 3:5)

Noisy (Acts 2:14)

Old-fashioned (I Cor. 15:1)

Pointed (Matt. 3:7) Lester Roloff would say, "Preachers should preach porcupine sermons so the people get the point!"

Quick-witted (I Kings 18:27)

Razor sharp (Acts 7:54)

Searching (John 8:7)

Tender and tremendous (Jer. 9:1)

Uncompromising (Acts 5:29)

Vehement (Mark 6:18)

Warlike (II Tim. 4:7)

X-raying (Heb. 4:12)

Yearning (Jer. 20:9)

Zealous (Acts 26:29)

Charles Spurgeon was to preach in the famed Agricultural Hall in London, England. Wanting to test the acoustics, he visited the mammoth auditorium during the day before the evening service. He stood on the platform, looked out across the empty building, lifted up his voice and quoted John 1:29: "Behold the Lamb of God, which taketh away the sin of the world." A man working in the ceiling heard Mr. Spurgeon's voice and came under conviction. He climbed down his ladder, went home, knelt beside his bed and gave his heart to the Lord Jesus Christ.

Conversion takes place when the Word of God is enthusiastically believed and excitingly preached.

II. THE LIGHT GOES OUT WHEN THERE'S NO BROTHERHOOD PRACTICED

"Honour all men. Love the brotherhood. Fear God. Honour the king."—I Pet. 2:17.

There is no relationship in life that is left outside the sphere of Christian responsibility.

Loving the brotherhood is not a choice; the believer is obligated to love the members of his spiritual family. Only two times in the Bible do we find the word "brotherhood" (Zech. 11:14 and I Pet. 2:17), and in both cases it means "brotherly affection."

You are a brother to anyone who is saved. Because we are saved, we are both of the same family. We ought to love one another, appreciate one another and fellowship one with another, because we are brethren in the same body.

Illumination does not mean that all the brothers and sisters have the same likes and dislikes, the same personalities or the same makeup.

You are different from me; I am different from you. In fact, I am at the point in my life where I am follicularly impaired; the trip *to* the barbershop is longer than the stay *at* the barbershop.

Here are some facts about "brotherhood" that show why it must be the order of the day.

1. Brotherly love is to be considerate. "Be kindly affectioned one to another with brotherly love; in honour preferring one another" (Rom. 12:10).

Brotherly affection says, "It is preferable that you go first, and it is acceptable for me to go last." It is sensitive to the needs of others; it is guarded in what it says and does.

2. Brotherly love is to be communicated. "But as touching brotherly love ye need not that I write unto you: for ye yourselves are taught of God to love one another" (I Thess. 4:9).

103

In the classroom of Christianity, the believer sits at his desk and listens to God as He lectures before His blackboard on the great subject of loving one another. No matter what faults and flaws they have, we are to love other Christians.

3. Brotherly love is to be continued. "Let brotherly love continue" (Heb. 13:1).

Too often spiritual giants in the home become spiritual pygmies in church, and that's not how it should be. Where Christian love does not cease, conflict in the local church does not begin.

Brothers in Christ should be able to iron out any problem that arises between them. That doesn't mean that we have to agree on everything. We simply decide to stay in the same family and work together toward the same goal.

Every community needs a church with a light that serves as a brightly burning beacon.

General Marquis de Lafayette was the French soldier and statesman who helped General George Washington when the thirteen colonies were fighting for their freedom. After the war, he returned to France. When he visited America in 1824, an old soldier went up to him and said, "Do you remember me?"

"No," he said.

"Do you remember the frosts and the snows of Valley Forge?"

"I shall never forget them," he replied.

"One bitterly cold night," said the soldier, "you were doing the rounds. You came upon a sentry who was thinly clothed and freezing to death. You took his gun and said, 'Go to my quarters. There you'll find clothes, a blanket and a fire. After warming yourself, bring the blanket to me; meanwhile I'll keep guard for you.'

"When the soldier returned, you cut the blanket into two pieces—one piece you kept, and you gave the other piece to the sentry." By now tears were running down the cheeks of that old soldier. "Here is the other half of that blanket, for I am that sentry."

If we aren't willing to split our blankets in two and share them with others, the light will go out in the house of God.

III. THE LIGHT GOES OUT WHEN THERE IS NO BURDEN PRONOUNCED

"Therefore watch, and remember, that by the space of three years I ceased not to warn every one night and day with tears."— Acts 20:31.

The word *pronounced* means "something easily seen or something effectively stated."

The apostle Paul witnessed and wept every day for three years over those who were without the Lord Jesus Christ in Ephesus—not days and months, but years. Morning and evening, day and night, he witnessed and wept for those who were lost.

Every tear he shed was a tender sermon that screamed, "I want you to be saved!"

We need to know that the light will go out in the house of God when there is no pronounced burden.

Jude 22 says, "And of some have compassion, making a difference."

You can't determine the depth of a church's desire to see

souls saved by measuring the height of the steeple or by feeling the padding of the pews. Their zeal for souls is recognized through several things.

Zeal is seen at the altar. Something is wrong when a Christian never feels the need to go to the altar to do business with God. We live in a wicked world and rub shoulders with the lost, so how can we not shed tears on the altar, praying for their souls? A church's desire must be to see the world brought to Christ.

The tract rack will testify to a church's zeal for souls. The tract rack is a spiritual ammunition depot, because tracts are Bible bullets for the harvest. It is a crime when tracts lose their print and the paper becomes dog-eared and yellow because they've been on the rack for so long.

Our pockets and purses ought to be filled with Bible bullets waiting to be distributed to the lost.

One day my mother called me and said, "John, I want to know if you think I was right to do something that I've done. I stuck about ten or twenty gospel tracts along the liquor aisle at the grocery store. Should I have done that?"

I said, "Keep at it!"

Tracts are not to stay in the tract rack.

A church's zeal is evidenced in its visitation and soul-winning programs. You need to attend and support these programs.

This church had seven souls saved this past weekend because people went out soul winning every day. You'll never get *any* that you don't go after, you'll never get *all* that you do go after, but you'll always get *some* if you'll just go.

If a church has a zeal for souls, it will strongly support missionaries. Every Christian should give to missions, over and above his tithe. If this bothers you, then blame the Bible, because tithing and giving to missions are in the Bible!

Don't let your work in church services take the place of your mission work—that is what you do beyond the walls of your church.

Why are you bored when the pastor reads a missions letter; why do you keep looking at your watch when a report is given by a missionary; why do you sigh when a missionary gets up to speak? Could it be because you're not giving to missions? If you don't give to missions, that shows you don't care about missions. Of course you're bored and dread to see missionaries come to your church. Anyone who thinks missionaries are second-class servants, less important than his own Christian service, is likely to be stingy—a spiritual tightwad who won't give a dime toward the cause of Christ in world evangelism.

During a four-day revival meeting I was conducting in Flint, Michigan in 2001, a lady asked me to pray with her that her next-door neighbor would come to that meeting and come to Christ. This woman had a slight mental handicap, and she spoke with a speech impediment.

The next night she had someone with her, and this person also had a bit of a mental handicap. At the end of the service, they stayed in their pew, holding one another and weeping uncontrollably. I assumed that one of them had a serious problem. Eventually they came to me, and the lady who had asked me to pray said, "Dr. Hamblin, this is the next-door neighbor that we prayed for last night, and she just got saved. We are crying because we are so happy that she's saved!"

Then I started to weep, and I thought, *I wonder who really has the handicap.*

When a church does not proclaim a Bible, when it does not practice brotherhood, when it does not have a pronounced burden, the lamp of God will go out in the temple of the Lord.

What a tragedy!

Chapter 10

YOUR TEARS IN
GOD'S BOTTLE

"Be merciful unto me, O God: for man would swallow me up;
he fighting daily oppresseth me.

"Mine enemies would daily swallow me up: for they be many
that fight against me, O thou most High.

"What time I am afraid, I will trust in thee.

"In God I will praise his word, in God I have put my trust; I
will not fear what flesh can do unto me.

"Every day they wrest my words: all their thoughts are
against me for evil.

"They gather themselves together, they hide themselves, they
mark my steps, when they wait for my soul.

"Shall they escape by iniquity? in thine anger cast down the
people, O God.

"Thou tellest my wanderings: put thou my tears into thy
bottle: are they not in thy book?

"When I cry unto thee, then shall mine enemies turn back: this
I know; for God is for me.

"In God will I praise his word: in the LORD will I praise
his word.

"In God have I put my trust: I will not be afraid what man
can do unto me.

"Thy vows are upon me, O God: I will render praises unto thee.

109

"For thou hast delivered my soul from death: wilt not thou deliver my feet from falling, that I may walk before God in the light of the living?"—Ps. 56.

This psalm was penned when King David had to seek refuge among the Philistines from his own countrymen. While David is telling us about how God declares the steps of our wanderings, he also shares with us that God keeps our tears.

Please notice that it is *our* tears, but it is *God's* bottle.

The Word of God teaches us that there are three reasons why we shed tears.

1. We shed tears because of physical pain. "When the unclean spirit had torn him, and cried with a loud voice, he came out of him" (Mark 1:26).

2. We shed tears because of emotional pain. "When Esau heard the words of his father, he cried with a great and exceeding bitter cry, and said unto his father, Bless me, even me also, O my father" (Gen. 27:34).

3. We shed tears because of spiritual pain. "Moses cried unto the LORD, saying, What shall I do unto this people? they be almost ready to stone me" (Exod. 17:4).

"Put thou my tears into thy bottle" may be an allusion to an ancient custom in which mourners preserved their falling tears in a small bottle to be placed in the tombs of deceased family and friends as a memorial of the survivors' affection. Archaeologists, when discovering ancient graves, have unearthed these tear bottles, and I think that is what David is alluding to in this passage.

We have never shed a tear that God has not caught in His bottle and saved it.

"Thy bottle" says some wonderful things about God. It's not just some old container, but a *bottle* that God uses to catch our tears.

I. GOD SEES

"The eyes of the LORD run to and fro throughout the whole earth."—II Chron. 16:9.

God had given King Asa a majestic and mighty victory over the Ethiopian king, but then King Baasha from the northern kingdom of Israel came against him. Asa bribed the king of Syria to break his alliance with Baasha and help him instead. But God came to Asa by way of Hanani and rebuked the king for trusting man instead of God. It was in that rebuke that we find the expression, "The eyes of the LORD run to and fro throughout the whole earth."

Sometimes we need this same rebuke. We face difficulties, and we whine and whimper and act like Asa did. God sees all that is happening to us, and instead of having a bad spirit, we ought to take comfort in the fact that God is watching and knows all about the situation.

When Christians face the storms of life, they can be certain that Christ sees them, that He is aware of everything and that He doesn't miss any details of what's going on in their lives.

Mark 6:48 says, "He saw them toiling in rowing; for the wind was contrary unto them."

Jesus had told the disciples to enter into a ship and to cross the Sea of Galilee, a sea where storms suddenly break out. They didn't get very far from shore before the storm clouds began to gather; then the rain fell, the lightning flashed, and the thunder crashed. They were laboring against the storm when "He saw them."

Maybe your sea is rough, and you are having trouble staying afloat. You can't seem to stay ahead of the storm; the water is splashing into your boat, the wind is blowing you all about, and you are about to sink. But God sees you and knows where you are and what you are going through. You will not shed one tear that God will not catch and put in His tear bottle.

One night after a service where I was preaching in Arizona, a lady came up to me and said, "You said tonight that God is always good to the believer. My pastor says that, and I don't agree with either one of you. Recently my husband lost a very good job. We had everything that this world offers, and we've lost everything that was important to us. All we have are cheese sandwiches for breakfast, lunch and dinner! How can you say, 'God is always good to the believer'? I don't think so."

I said, "Sister, if it weren't for God, you wouldn't have cheese sandwiches!"

"The eyes of the LORD" see everything.

II. GOD STRENGTHENS

"It is God that girdeth me with strength, and maketh my way perfect."—Ps. 18:32.

Azar, the Hebrew word for "girdeth," means "to bind about." That's what God does—He binds us about. And when we see Him catching our tears, it means that God is strengthening us.

Where would we be if it weren't for the strength of God? His strength has brought us to this point, and it will take us to the next point. Whatever we face, we must face it with the undergirding, the strength, the might and the power of God Almighty.

I want to give you three tools that God uses to strengthen His children.

1. He uses the Holy Scriptures. "My soul melteth for heaviness: strengthen thou me according unto thy word" (Ps. 119:28).

You will never be a strong Christian if you are not a Bible-reading Christian. Not one day should pass in your life when you don't read the Word of God. You will not make it on the preacher's preaching alone; you need a daily encounter with the Word of the Living God.

2. He uses the saints. "Jonathan Saul's son arose, and went to David into the wood, and strengthened his hand in God" (I Sam. 23:16).

David was at the point spiritually where his strength was waning, but God used another saint to give David the spiritual wherewithal to go on.

Christians are supposed to strengthen one another.

I am weary of hearing what some Christians say to other Christians, even in jest. Christians are not to be stand-up comedians, and we need to be careful about what we say. We don't always know what others are going through, and what they need is for you to build them up, not pull them down. Too often an off-the-cuff comment is cruel and foolish rather than witty.

Young preachers and evangelists need to be strengthened.

When I first went into evangelism, several preachers

said, "You'll never make it. You can't be an evangelist! You've never been a pastor! How do you expect to do anything for God?" Wasn't that an encouraging way to talk to a young evangelist?

But God knew my heart, and He blessed my ministry. Now some of those same rascals have me in their churches for meetings, and they introduce me this way: "I always knew Dr. Hamblin would have an effective ministry, and I've always been right behind him." I want to say, "Liar, liar, pants on fire!"

We're in this thing together, and we need to strengthen one another.

3. He uses the Holy Spirit. "That he would grant you, according to the riches of his glory, to be strengthened with might by his Spirit in the inner man" (Eph. 3:16).

This Third Person of the Trinity lives in our bodies and abides in our souls, and we never take a step that He is not taking with us.

To strengthen us, God uses the Holy Scriptures, other saints and the Holy Spirit.

III. GOD WILL SOON ELIMINATE SORROW

"And God shall wipe away all tears from their eyes; and there shall be no more death, neither sorrow, nor crying, neither shall there be any more pain: for the former things are passed away."— Rev. 21:4.

"...And sorrow and sighing shall flee away."—Isa. 35:10.

One day we are going to say good-bye to heartache, to

sorrow, to burdens and to all that wrenches our soul.

It will be a happy hour for believers when the Heavenly Father wipes away all our tears once and for all .

Some of you reading this have a heavy burden and a broken heart. You may not understand what you are going through, but take courage, child of God; you'll not always weep or stain your pillows with your tears. There is coming a time when God will say, "No more weeping, child!"

Right after I got saved, I heard older people talking about going to Heaven. Tears welled up in their eyes, their voices choked with emotion, and I wondered, *Why do they act like that?*

I remember when God let my heart break for the first time. He showed me that in Heaven my heart will never break again. Then I knew why these dear folks were weeping.

Aren't you looking forward to the day when that burden you have for your unsaved wife won't be there? when the burden for wayward children won't be there? when that loved one lying on the bed of affliction will have a new body just as glorious and matchless and perfect as the body of Jesus? Oh, what a happy day!

Last night I had the wonderful privilege of driving Dr. Malone to a meeting—I wouldn't trade that privilege for a tent full of hundred dollar bills! I told him what I was going to preach, and then I asked him if he could give me a good illustration for my sermon. He said:

> I had a cousin whose name was Lloyd, and we grew up together on my grandfather's farm. One day Lloyd met an affluent, pretty young lady, and later they got married. They had everything, and his father-in-law taught him

the family business (he owned a chemical company).

One day Lloyd owned his own chemical company. But at the age of forty-two, he passed away very suddenly. I was asked to preach the funeral.

I flew my own plane back then, so I flew myself down to Louisiana. When I finished preaching, my aunt came to the casket and looked at her forty-two-year-old son and said, "Son, I'll see you in the morning." Then she turned and walked away.

Christian, think about the short span between the night and the morning. It will just be in the morning when God will wipe away our tears, and we will never, ever weep again.

I don't know what you are facing, but I do know that not one of your tears lands on the ground; they land in God's hands. And He moves those tears from His hands and puts them into your personal tear bottle.

Take heart, child of God, God will soon eliminate all sorrow.

Chapter 11

WHEN YOU DON'T KNOW
WHAT TO DO

"David and his men came to the city, and, behold, it was burned with fire; and their wives, and their sons, and their daughters, were taken captives.

"Then David and the people that were with him lifted up their voice and wept, until they had no more power to weep.

"And David's two wives were taken captives, Ahinoam the Jezreelitess, and Abigail the wife of Nabal the Carmelite.

"And David was greatly distressed; for the people spake of stoning him, because the soul of all the people was grieved, every man for his sons and for his daughters: but David encouraged himself in the LORD his God.

"And David said to Abiathar the priest, Ahimelech's son, I pray thee, bring me hither the ephod. And Abiathar brought thither the ephod to David.

"And David enquired at the LORD, saying, Shall I pursue after this troop? shall I overtake them? And he answered him, Pursue: for thou shalt surely overtake them, and without fail recover all.

"So David went, he and the six hundred men that were with him, and came to the brook Besor, where those that were left behind stayed.

"But David pursued, he and four hundred men: for two hundred

abode behind, which were so faint that they could not go over the brook Besor."—I Sam. 30:3–10.

There will be seasons in every saint's life when he will seek direction for his next step. It may be at the foot of a high mountain or the entrance of a low valley, but it is in these hard-moving hours that God desires to change your question marks into exclamation points.

There are times when we think we have more questions than there are answers. But we can go to the Word of God, the written voice of God, and see what David did when he didn't know what to do.

I. WHEN YOU DON'T KNOW WHAT TO DO, PRAY

"And David said to Abiathar the priest, Ahimelech's son, I pray thee, bring me hither the ephod. And Abiathar brought thither the ephod to David."—Vs. 7.

The writer tells us that the same minute David saw the empty city of Ziklag, smelled the smoke from the burning buildings, heard the weeping of the troops and sensed the violent uprising, he requested the priest to bring him the ephod.

The ephod was a portion of the high priest's garment that was in two pieces—one for the back and one for the front. The two pieces were joined by shoulder pieces which were continuations of the front piece. On the shoulder pieces were two precious stones, each having the names of six of the tribes of Israel. These stones were placed in gold settings which probably clasped the two pieces together. The ephod was fastened around the body by means of a girdle which was a portion of the front piece. The two pieces joined together speak of intercessory prayer.

David's first response was to pray, and when we don't know what to do, we ought to pray.

Psalm 18:6 says, "In my distress I called upon the LORD, and cried unto my God: he heard my voice out of his temple, and my cry came before him, even into his ears."

Too often when Christians face perplexing problems, stress or personal catastrophe, they pick up the phone and speed dial all of their friends and family. Don't you think that the great heart of our Heavenly Father is grieved when He watches His children talking to everyone and their dogs and cats about their difficulties and the decisions they need to make *before* they utter a single word to Him.

I have a dear preacher-friend who told me that once when he was going through some difficult situations, he picked up his phone to call me. But as soon as he started to dial my number, the Lord seemed to ask, "What about talking to Me?" He immediately hung up the phone, got down on his knees and told God all about it.

By the way, I'm not saying that he heard God's voice. When you got saved, the Third Person of the Trinity moved *into* your body—"the temple of God"—and He is not going to step *outside* your body to speak to you.

God does not speak to anybody out loud. He uses the sixty-six books that make up His one Book—that's His megaphone to your heart!

People tell me that they had a vision! But why would God use a vision, when He's already given us a Book full of verses?

I'm also not saying that there is something wrong with

talking to family and friends about problems, but before that first call, tell it to God.

During World War II, under a group of government buildings in Storys Gate off of White Hall, London, over one hundred fifty subterranean rooms were in daily use. Many people called these quarters "the hole."

Among these rooms were a map room with a great map of the world and its sea routes, a cabinet room where the enemy's strategy was debated by leading strategists, a telephone room and a key room for the purpose of holding regular communication with other rulers—and all of this was done in secret.

The great statesman Winston Churchill refused to call it "the hole"; instead he called it "the secret place."

When you don't have any idea what to do next, move to your secret place and communicate with the One who is listening with bended ear.

II. WHEN YOU DON'T KNOW WHAT TO DO, PURSUE

"And David enquired at the LORD, *saying, Shall I pursue after this troop? shall I overtake them? And he answered him, Pursue: for thou shalt surely overtake them, and without fail recover all."*—Vs. 8.

When the believer doesn't know what to do, he should not only pray; he should pursue.

It was while David was meeting with God that he was told to go after his family and his soldiers' families. God didn't leave any chance for David to misunderstand His direction; He made it crystal-clear: "Pursue."

Radaph, the Hebrew word for pursue, means "to run after." We are to pursue when we don't know what to do. There is only one direction for the Christian: forward. Don't put it in spiritual "park," because if you do, it won't be long until you put it in spiritual "reverse"; and, friend, that is the wrong direction.

Sometimes we sail *with* the wind, sometimes we sail *against* it, but we must never allow ourselves to drift or lie at anchor.

Even in the building of a new church house, there will be times when the people come to a crossroads where nothing works, nothing fits and nothing goes right. That's when church members need to say, "We're not going to stop! We're going to see this project through! We're going to pursue!"

There are several things that God desires the believer to follow after, no matter what problems arise.

1. He should follow after right living. "Hearken to me, ye that follow after righteousness, ye that seek the LORD: look unto the rock whence ye are hewn, and to the hole of the pit whence ye are digged" (Isa. 51:1).

Whenever the redeemed head toward right living, they will reach a close relationship with God.

2. He should follow after right loving. "Follow after charity [love]" (I Cor. 14:1).

Actions that are inspired by authentic admiration will always improve a home, a marriage or a church. But here's our big problem: we say, "If *they'll* act right, *we'll* act right. If *they* initiate affection, *we'll* return their affection." That is backwards! *We* are the ones who ought to initiate expressions of love in our home, in our church and in all of our relationships.

121

Too many Christians carry with them the same selfish mentality they had on the playground when they were in the fourth grade.

Right loving sometimes means that you have to extend your hand first, that you have to be the first one to speak, that you have to be the encourager.

3. He should follow after right lifting. "Let us therefore follow after the things which make for peace, and things wherewith one may edify another" (Rom. 14:19).

Every Christian needs to be uplifted and encouraged by another believer. If you do things to uplift and encourage others, God will see to it that others will be there to uplift and encourage you—that's not the motivation, but that's how it works.

A cheerful and encouraging word spoken by an English naval officer saved a sailor from disgrace and a dishonorable discharge. During a fierce engagement with an enemy ship, the volleys from a number of firearms so frightened the fourteen-year-old sailor that he trembled and almost fainted.

The officer came beside him and said, "Courage, my boy! You will recover in a minute or two. I was just like you when I went into my first battle."

Afterward the young man said, "It was as if an angel had come and given me new strength."

Both officer and sailor were under the same fire, but, even with all his other pressing duties, the officer took a moment to encourage the young man.

When you don't know what to do, pursue.

III. WHEN YOU DON'T KNOW WHAT TO DO, PUT YOUR LIFE IN THE PATH OF PROVIDENCE

"So David went, he and the six hundred men that were with him, and came to the brook Besor, where those that were left behind stayed."—I Sam. 30:9.

The author of I Samuel tells us that immediately after David got the green light from God, he gathered his troops and went out to rescue his family.

Not very far down the winding road of divine guidance, David found a refreshed guide, a relaxed enemy, a reunited family, a retrieved possession and a rewarded heart. But none of these things would have come about if it had not been for that small three-word phrase: "So David went."

When we don't know what to do, we must put ourselves in the path of providence. Romans 8:28 says, "And we know that all things work together for good to them that love God, to them who are the called according to his purpose."

Christians will never know that what they were up against was for their spiritual good if they never move from their spiritual recliner. "So David went," and you too have to get up and get going.

A preacher brother contracted a rare virus that attacks the body's nervous system and leaves one completely paralyzed. It does not kill, but it weakens the body to the point that other infections, mainly pneumonia, can cause death. The specialist who was treating him had seen only three cases of this virus.

For over five months he was on a ventilator, in and out of

the hospital, and he almost died. His mind was still clear and sharp, but he needed a card with an alphabet on it to communicate. His family would point to each letter, and he would move his eyes when they came to the letter he wanted to use. Then they put the letters together to make words.

I visited with him and prayed with him. I never went into that hospital room without a broken heart. One day we received a card from his wife; in the thank-you note was a small, white piece of paper on which was written:

He Maketh No Mistake

My Father's way may twist and turn;
  My heart may throb and ache.
But in my soul I'm glad I know
  He maketh no mistake.

My cherished plans may go astray;
  My hopes may fade away.
But still I'll trust my Lord to lead,
  For He doth know the way.

Tho' night be dark and it may seem
  That day will never break,
I'll pin my faith, my all in Him;
  He maketh no mistake.

There's so much now I cannot see—
  My eyesight's far too dim—
But come what may, I'll simply trust
  And leave it all to Him.

For by and by the mist will lift,
  And plain it all He'll make;
Through all the way, tho' dark to me,
  He made not one mistake.

A. M. Overton

When you put your life in the path of divine providence, there is a confidence that "He maketh no mistake."

Christian, put your life in that path.

Every one of us will come to a time when we don't know what to do. That is not the time for a pity party, giving up or saying, "Whoa!"

When you don't know what to do, pray—that's what David did. When you don't know what to do, pursue—that's what David did. When you don't know what to do, put your life in the path of providence—that's what David did. And when David had done all these things, his situation was turned completely around. It will be the same for you.

Chapter 12

THE MOST WONDERFUL
VERSE ON PRAYER

"Call unto me, and I will answer thee, and shew thee great and mighty things, which thou knowest not."—Jer. 33:3.

The Bible is filled with towering verses that challenge believers to petition their Heavenly Father. I believe that Jeremiah 33:3 is the Mount Everest of prayer. There is no other Scripture which dares an individual to climb the heights of supplication like this verse, the most wonderful verse on prayer.

Every Christian should have one verse that is near and dear to his heart. I still recall when, as a new convert, I saw this most marvelous Scripture. I said to myself, *There it is— my life's verse!*

Why would an evangelist choose that verse? Because God gives us a pattern, a plan, for revival: "If my people, which are called by my name, shall humble themselves, and pray, and seek my face, and turn from their wicked ways; then will I hear from heaven, and will forgive their sin, and will heal their land" (II Chron. 7:14); and there in that blueprint is the word "pray."

We are taught three things from Jeremiah 33:3 about the great matter of prayer.

I. THE INVITATION

"Call unto me...."

The believer learns about the invitation to prayer from this verse. Here the Heavenly Father uses an appeal to encourage His children to bring their petitions to Him.

Prayer was not man's idea; prayer was God's idea. The psalmist Asaph wrote that prayer was requested by God: "Call upon me in the day of trouble: I will deliver thee, and thou shalt glorify me" (Ps. 50:15).

Our lives would be much less disquieted, disturbed and distressed if we would only respond to the invitation that comes from Heaven's throne.

Joseph Scriven, a great hymn writer, must have had this truth upon his heart when he picked up the songwriter's pen and wrote the heart-penetrating words to "What a Friend We Have in Jesus":

> **What a Friend we have in Jesus,**
> **All our sins and griefs to bear!**
> **What a privilege to carry**
> **Ev'rything to God in prayer!**
> **Oh, what peace we often forfeit,**
> **Oh, what needless pain we bear,**
> **All because we do not carry**
> **Ev'rything to God in prayer!**

There are two kinds of people who have problems: people who know they have problems and people who don't know they have problems. You may have a broken heart this morning, but you can give that broken heart to God because of His wonderful invitation to pray.

There is in the Word of God a heart-gripping illustration

of a believer who went to God with her problem.

Hannah was unable to bear a child. She did not know the joys of motherhood, of feeling a little child's arms around her neck or feeling the heartbeat of the one she carried for a number of months. But Hannah went to the house of God and carried her problem to Him by way of prayer.

Hannah had a problem, but she didn't run *from* church; she ran *to* church. She knew that the house of God was a place of hope and a place of help.

By the way, you will not find hope or help on the job or at your grandmother's house or at your friend's house, but you will find help in the living God.

Hannah went to church, and she prayed. She was criticized and told she was doing the wrong thing, and she found opposition from those who were upset with what she did. But she kept on praying.

After the normal length of time, God gave a baby boy to barren Hannah; and she called him Samuel, a name meaning "asked of God."

We should follow the wonderful example of Sister Hannah by bringing all of our problems to God.

One of Albert Einstein's neighbors noticed that her ten-year-old daughter often visited the scientist's house. The child explained:

> I was having trouble with my arithmetic homework. I heard that a big mathematician, who was also a very good man, lived right up the street. One day I knocked on his door and asked him for help with my homework.
>
> He was very willing, and he explained everything

very well. When I left that first day, he said, "Whenever you come to a problem that is difficult in your math homework, just come and talk to me."

Christian, aren't you glad that the child of God is just as welcome to go to God with everything upon his heart, everything in his life, as that little girl was in going to Albert Einstein's house?

II. THE INCENTIVE

"...I will answer thee...."

The believer learns about the incentive of prayer from this verse. Here the Heavenly Father uses motivation to encourage His children to bring their petitions to Him.

If you don't think we ought to motivate people to do things, take it up with God. If you don't think we ought to hang a carrot on a stick in front of people, take it up with God. He gives us a great big spiritual carrot—this verse—and it is the motivation, the incentive to pray.

The Lord Jesus Christ taught His disciples that prayer was answered by God.

"Ask, and it shall be given you; seek, and ye shall find; knock, and it shall be opened unto you:

"For every one that asketh receiveth; and he that seeketh findeth; and to him that knocketh it shall be opened."—Matt. 7:7,8.

There is nothing that would transform the prayer life of the average Christian like the realization that God will answer prayer for him!

Charles Haddon Spurgeon, the "Prince of Preachers," once said, "Prayer pulls the rope down below, and the great bell rings above in the ears of God. Some scarcely stir the bell, for they pray so languidly; others give an occasional pluck at the rope; but he who communicates with Heaven is the man who grabs the rope boldly and pulls it continuously with all his might."

We should pray and ask God for His blessing and power and for revival because of the incentive of prayer.

Prayer is not an exercise in futility or a waste of time. You are not spinning your wheels or beating your head against a wall when you pray. When you pray, you have incentive that God is going to do something.

There are three things that assure the believer that prayer will be answered.

1. We have assurance from the promises of the Bible. "For all the promises of God in him are yea, and in him Amen, unto the glory of God by us" (II Cor. 1:20).

The promises of the Word of God are the child of God's spiritual credit card—you cannot *max it out*, it is always accepted, and it will never put your credit on hold.

2. We have assurance from the power of God. "But if thou wilt go, do it, be strong for the battle: God shall make thee fall before the enemy: for God hath power to help, and to cast down" (II Chron. 25:8).

The power of God—the omnipotence of the Heavenly Father—is the wheelbarrow that carries the answer to His children's requests. We serve a powerful God. We serve a magnificent God. We serve the all-time, undisputed, undefeated Champion!

When you talk to God, He turns the impossible into possible, the hard into easy, and the difficult into delightful.

3. We have assurance from the past testimony of believers. "Because he hath inclined his ear unto me, therefore will I call upon him as long as I live" (Ps. 116:2).

We can believe that prayer will be answered because of the past testimony of other believers. The statements from Christians of the past ought to inspire Christians in the present to spend time on their knees.

Oh, that every believer would be assured that prayer will be answered because of the promises of the Bible, the power of God and the past testimony of believers!

At a prayer meeting, a little boy requested prayer that the Lord would help his sister to read the Bible. As soon as someone began to pray for the little boy's sister, he got up and went out. Everyone thought he was rude.

The next day the pastor saw the little boy on the street. He said, "Why did you ask the church to pray for your sister and then jump up and run out? You shouldn't have done that!"

The little boy said, "I just wanted to run and see my sister reading the Bible for the first time."

When we pray, we ought to pray like this little boy—looking for the answer and knowing that God is going to do something.

III. THE INCREDIBLE

"...I will...shew thee great and mighty things, which thou knowest not."

Here the Heavenly Father uses extraordinary things to encourage His children to bring their petitions to Him.

The word *great* in the Hebrew language means "exceedingly"; the word *mighty* means "strong."

The apostle Paul wrote to the saints in Ephesus that prayer—talking to God, supplication—accomplishes remarkable things for God. "Now unto him that is able to do exceeding abundantly above all that we ask or think, according to the power that worketh in us" (Eph 3:20).

It is a heartbreaking fact that the vast majority of Christians pray like God is either broke and in the poorhouse or bedfast in the nursing home.

We pray like God is hooked up to a life-support system, like He is standing in a bread line, like he owns only a thrift store, like He is on the last part of His pension. No! God has promised incredible things if we will just talk to Him!

There are innumerable illustrations and incidents where a person or a group of people asked God for things of incredible magnitude and He came through.

The healing of bodies comes, in God's sovereign will, through prayer, and you don't have to call on anyone but God. He can work it out.

I wouldn't be preaching this morning if it weren't for God's healing touch. Doctors have told me on occasion that I had illnesses that were ministry threatening—that would put me on hold or stop me completely. But I prayed, and some prayer warriors prayed for me, and God turned it around.

Through prayer, there is the reclaiming of backsliders. I was in a service where a Christian walked down the aisle and knelt at the altar with his parents and God did something in the deep recesses of their hearts. It happened because of prayer.

Through prayer, churches are started. A pastor said to

me, "God has put it upon my heart to start a church," and five years later a soul-saving station is preaching the Word, holding revivals, changing lives and lifting up the Gospel of Jesus Christ.

Prayer is instrumental in the saving of a soul. All answers to prayer, though marvelous and mighty, pale in comparison to answered prayer for the salvation of a lost soul. "For whosoever shall call upon the name of the Lord shall be saved" (Rom. 10:13).

Many years ago, in a service where the Bible was preached and the sweet Spirit of God did His divine work in my heart, I realized that I was a heartbeat from Hell and a breath from the bottomless pit. As the invitation hymn was sung, I walked down an aisle, knelt at an altar and was gloriously born into the family of God.

Wouldn't it be wonderful if someone reading this book was healed according to God's sovereign will; I'm not talking about going through a healing line but going to God in prayer, knowing that He can do anything.

Wouldn't it be wonderful if some backslider reading this message came back home.

Wouldn't it be wonderful if some young man, touched by this sermon, was not only called by God to preach, but also accepted the call of his sovereign Father.

Wouldn't it be wonderful if these words led some people to stagger out of the darkness of sin and into the delightful embrace of the Saviour to be saved.

Psalm 81:10 says, "I am the LORD thy God, which brought thee out of the land of Egypt: open thy mouth wide, and I will fill it." This truth should cause every one of us to return to praying for the hardest of unsaved loved ones, the biggest of material needs and the coldest of Christian friends.

On one occasion, a courtier asked Alexander the Great for some financial aid. The great leader told him to go to his treasurer and ask for whatever amount he needed.

Later, the treasurer appeared before Alexander and said, "The man asked for an enormous amount of money, and I hesitated to pay out so much."

"Give him what he asked for," replied the great conqueror. "He has treated me like a king in his asking, and I shall treat him like a king in my giving."

Oh, that when we pray we would realize to whom we are praying—the King!

> **Thou art coming to a King;**
> **Large petitions with thee bring,**
> **For His grace and power are such**
> **That no one can ask too much.**

"Call unto me, and I will answer thee, and shew thee great and mighty things, which thou knowest not."

This most wonderful verse on prayer is so powerful that it will help the Christian to come to God and get things *from* Heaven, and it will help the unsaved to get saved and get *to* Heaven.

Chapter 13

"SING THE LORD'S SONG IN A STRANGE LAND"

"By the rivers of Babylon, there we sat down, yea, we wept, when we remembered Zion.

"We hanged our harps upon the willows in the midst thereof.

"For there they that carried us away captive required of us a song; and they that wasted us required of us mirth, saying, Sing us one of the songs of Zion.

"How shall we sing the LORD'S *song in a strange land?*

"If I forget thee, O Jerusalem, let my right hand forget her cunning.

"If I do not remember thee, let my tongue cleave to the roof of my mouth; if I prefer not Jerusalem above my chief joy.

"Remember, O LORD, *the children of Edom in the day of Jerusalem; who said, Rase it, rase it, even to the foundation thereof.*

"O daughter of Babylon, who art to be destroyed; happy shall he be, that rewardeth thee as thou hast served us.

"Happy shall he be, that taketh and dasheth thy little ones against the stones."—Ps. 137.

The world has every right to request a song from the church. Only believers have the ability to sing in the deepest valley while facing the darkest storm. The unsaved miss the most meaningful music ever heard, when the saved are silenced.

In our text, we see the nation of Israel exiled in the land of Babylon. We read in this passage about their bewilderment because of the Babylonians' request, "Sing us one of the songs of Zion." But the ungodly expect the godly to have a melody upon their lips.

Someone has said, "Israel's temple music had a reputation even among the heathen people of Central Asia. It seemed natural that the sacred words and music which had for ages set forth the worship of the one true God should furnish a more refined amusement for the cultured pagans who had trodden down the sanctuary and enslaved God's people."

When lost people are around Christians, they should be aware that we have a song, but the average child of God doesn't have that heavenly melody. All the world misses a blessing when the church has lost her song.

There are three songs that the sinner needs to hear sung by the saint.

I. THE SONG OF DELIVERANCE

The unsaved should hear the saved sing the song of deliverance.

"Then sang Moses and the children of Israel this song unto the LORD, and spake, saying, I will sing unto the LORD, for he hath triumphed gloriously: the horse and his rider hath he thrown into the sea."—Exod. 15:1.

Immediately after Israel's great victory over Pharaoh and the Egyptian army at the Red Sea, they sang a song of deliverance, a song of *relief.* Verse 11 is without question the most exciting verse of the song, because it points to the One who brought about this victory in the past and will bring about other victories in the present and in the future: "Who is like unto thee, O LORD, among the gods? who is like thee, glorious in holiness, fearful in praises, doing wonders?"

Never forget that deliverance is an amazing event that is attributed to an infinite God, not to finite man.

We need to sing the song of deliverance: "I sought the LORD, and he heard me, and delivered me from all my fears" (Ps. 34:4).

When God saves a lost loved one, meets a large financial need or returns a wayward child to the fold of the family, we should begin to sing a song of deliverance, a song of *rescue.*

You cannot sing if you don't have a song. I'm not talking about a song that comes from a hymnal, but a song that comes from the soul, for that is a song that the Lord has given you.

The songwriter P. P. Bliss was listening to an evangelist preach from the text, "But that which ye have already hold fast till I come" (Rev. 2:25). The evangelist told the story of a small force of Union soldiers who were guarding a great quantity of supplies. They were surrounded and hard-pressed by a greatly superior Confederate force.

Finally, Confederate General French demanded that the Union troops surrender. At that very moment, the troops saw in the distance a signal from General Sherman on a hill some miles away: "Hold the fort. I'm coming. Sherman."

The story so captivated Mr. Bliss' interest that he could not retire that evening until he had completed both the text and the music for a rousing song, the third verse of which is:

> **See the glorious banner waving!**
> **Hear the trumpet blow!**
> **In our Leader's name we'll triumph**
> **Over ev'ry foe.**
>
> **"Hold the fort, for I am coming,"**
> **Jesus signals still;**
> **Wave the answer back to Heaven,**
> **"By Thy grace we will."**

Christian, you may be only twenty-four hours from a Red Sea rescue, so just hold the fort—it won't be very long until you, like the Israelites, are singing a song of deliverance.

II. THE SONG OF DEITY

The unsaved should hear the saved sing the song of deity.

"Now will I sing to my wellbeloved a song of my beloved touching his vineyard."—Isa. 5:1.

The prophet Isaiah tells us that he sang a melody about the Lord and His tender care for the nation of Israel. This happy tune, however, soon turned into a sad tune because of the rebellion of the people.

A song about Jesus ought to be on our lips continually— a song about the Master, a song about the Son of God, a song about the Saviour of the world, a song about the King of Kings and Lord of Lords.

I'm not talking about a song that has the rhythm and tempo of those you might hear in the saloons or honky-tonks of the world, but a song that only a Christian can sing—a song about Jesus. Oh, that the world would hear a song from our lips about Him!

There are several proofs that point to the deity of the Lord Jesus Christ.

1. We see His deity in his message. "The officers answered, Never man spake like this man" (John 7:46). The lessons that fell from the lips of Jesus still shape men's lives today. The things that Jesus said and did centuries ago still move men's hearts tonight.

2. We see His deity in his miracles. "Jesus went forth, and saw a great multitude, and was moved with compassion toward them, and he healed their sick" (Matt. 14:14). Only God could cool a fevered brow, straighten a crooked limb and pull the dead back from the tomb—only God!

An old, converted drunk was once asked in a jeering tone, "Have you ever seen Jesus turn water into wine? Have you ever seen Jesus turn stones into bread?"

With tears in his eyes, he answered, "No, but I've seen Jesus turn liquor into a happy home with a paycheck for clothing and shoes for my wife and children. I've seen that!"

3. We see His deity in his miraculous resurrection. "He is not here, but is risen: remember how he spake unto you when he was yet in Galilee." (Luke 24:6).

Buddha is in the grave. Muhammad is in the grave. Joseph Smith, the founder of the Mormons, is in the grave. The founder of the Jehovah's Witnesses, Charles Taze Russell, is in the grave.

Mary Baker Glover Patterson Eddy is in the grave. She founded the Christian Science movement—which is neither Christian nor scientific. I am told that at her request they put a phone in her casket, because she felt that after she died she would be able to pick up the phone in the grave and call home. However, every month her phone bill reads a big, fat zero!

But let's walk into a garden toward a tomb where a great stone was rolled across the entrance when the body was placed there. Look! The stone has been rolled away. Peer within the dark shadows of the tomb. Are there any human remains inside?

Was this a vacant grave? Was this a virgin grave? Oh, no. I hear an angel say, "This is a victorious grave." Victorious? Yes, because Jesus stepped out of it!

The stone wasn't rolled away so *Jesus* could get *out;* it was rolled away so *we* could look *in* and see that He is not there.

Jesus' miraculous resurrection ought to bless and thrill your heart.

There is not a chorus in the world that can do what one hymn does to our hearts. Don't get me wrong, anything— including music—that lifts itself above preaching is not of God. I love music, I love singing, I'm married to a very talented musician, but music cannot take the place of the preaching of the Word of God. And whenever preaching is diminished in a church, that church is going the wrong direction in a hurry.

Fanny Crosby, J. Wilbur Chapman, Martin Luther, Charles Wesley, Dr. John R. Rice and others wrote hymns that we ought to sing in the house of God.

I was in a meeting recently where for two nights we didn't sing a single hymn. And what was worse, the preacher had moved the pulpit from the platform down to the first step above the auditorium floor. I was told they did so in order to have room for the gospel band.

"We needed more room for the steel guitar, the drum sets, the electric piano and the acoustic guitar," the preacher said without batting an eye.

Now, help me here. Does your Bible talk about having a gospel band in the pulpit? Yes, it's in the charismatic movement and in contemporary church services, but it should not be in our fundamental, independent Baptist churches!

The hymn "All Hail the Power" has many interesting stories attached to it. I think the greatest is told by E. P. Scott, a pioneer missionary to India.

One day he was ambushed by a murderous band of tribesmen who were closing in on him with spears. On impulse, he took out his violin and began to play and sing this hymn. When he reached the words "Lord of all," to his surprise, every spear lowered; many of the tribesmen were moved to tears.

Mr. Scott spent the remaining years of his life teaching and ministering God's love and redemption to these people.

Who knows how many unbelievers would lower their spears of unbelief and rejection if the believer would only sing the song of deity.

III. THE SONG OF DEPENDENCE

Not only should the unsaved hear the song of deliverance and the song of deity, but they should also hear the song of dependence.

"And at midnight Paul and Silas prayed, and sang praises unto God: and the prisoners heard them."—Acts 16:25.

143

The physician Luke tells us that right after Paul and Silas had been stripped and beaten and shoved into a prison, they sang the song of dependence, a song of reliance upon Someone who was greater than they were.

How could these two preachers have a melody of praise while in prison? They had total trust in and total dependence upon God; therefore, they had a song for any circumstance.

Most Christians have a song when the bills are paid, when the evangelist hasn't skinned their hide or when their in-laws are happy with them. Their song depends on what is going on around them instead of what's going on inside them. If you can only sing when things on the outside are going well, you'll never have a song that the world needs to hear. The song on the inside must move *you* before it will influence the unbeliever.

Psalm 37:5 says, "Commit thy way unto the LORD; trust also in him; and he shall bring it to pass." The believer who will trust wholly in Him can withstand any storm; and in the middle of the night, he will lie upon his bed resting, trusting and singing the song of dependence.

In a revival meeting many years ago, a woman got up and sang before I was to preach. She had a smile on her face, and it just seemed like the song radiated from her soul. Her singing blessed many hearts; in fact, it moved me to tears.

After the service, the pastor and I were having a bite to eat, and he told me this story about that dear lady.

Her son was addicted to mind-and-body-destroying chemicals, and just recently he asked his mother and father for money. They said, "No. You are an addict, and you will spend the money on drugs."

The boy became enraged. One night he hid in the garage, waiting for his father to get off his night-shift job. Early the next morning as his father stood on the porch and put his door key in the lock, a shot rang out from the garage. The father fell dead on his doorstep—murdered by the hand of his own son.

The father's body was put in the grave; the son was put in prison. Nevertheless, the mother continues singing for the Lord.

Listening to that woman sing, I would never have guessed what she was going through, the heartache she was feeling. She simply stood and sang her song of testimony with the touch of God upon her heart and the words of her soul in the song of dependence upon her Heavenly Father.

Dr. Oswald J. Smith relates the following account regarding the writing of his song, "God Understands."

My youngest sister and her husband were missionaries in Peru. As they were preparing for their first furlough, her husband was killed instantly in an automobile accident just before they were to set sail for home.

My sister, a widow at twenty-six, came home to Toronto. It was heart wrenching to see her step off the train with her two fatherless, young sons.

To her I dedicated "God Understands," because she understood that He understood before she left South America.

> **God understands your heartache;**
> **He knows the bitter pain.**
> **Oh, trust Him in the darkness;**
> **You cannot trust in vain.**

He understands your longing;
Your deepest grief He shares.
Then let Him bear your burden;
He understands and cares.

The song of dependence—Christian, aren't you glad that when you count on God, no matter the circumstance, you can sing a song that others who don't count on Him can never sing?

The unsaved wanted a song from God's children in the Babylonian days, and the world in our day wants to hear a song from Christians as well.

In this "strange land," do you have a song of deliverance, a song of deity and a song of dependence? Oh, that the unsaved world would hear "one of the songs of Zion"!

Chapter 14

THE PRODIGAL WHO

STAYED HOME

"Now his elder son was in the field: and as he came and drew nigh to the house, he heard musick and dancing.

"And he called one of the servants, and asked what these things meant.

"And he said unto him, Thy brother is come; and thy father hath killed the fatted calf, because he hath received him safe and sound.

"And he was angry, and would not go in: therefore came his father out, and intreated him.

"And he answering said to his father, Lo, these many years do I serve thee, neither transgressed I at any time thy commandment: and yet thou never gavest me a kid, that I might make merry with my friends:

"But as soon as this thy son was come, which hath devoured thy living with harlots, thou hast killed for him the fatted calf.

"And he said unto him, Son, thou art ever with me, and all that I have is thine.

"It was meet that we should make merry, and be glad: for this thy brother was dead, and is alive again; and was lost, and is found."—Luke 15:25–32.

Prodigals are found not only in a foreign country but also in a father's house. It is possible for a Christian to sing in the choir, serve in the Sunday school class, work a bus route or sit in the church and still be spiritually a thousand miles from God.

There are two prodigal sons in this story: "A certain man had two sons" (vs. 11). In our text we are introduced to the bad behavior of the backslidden elder brother.

There is the younger son who is *away* from home and away from his father, and there is the second son who is *at* home and away from his father. G. Campbell Morgan said:

The account of the elder brother reveals the possibility of living in the father's home and still failing to understand the father's heart.

A Christian can attend every service in a fundamental, independent, Bible-believing church and still be in an awful, backslidden condition.

Many Christians are of the mistaken opinion: "If I can just keep from committing a major sin, I must be close to Christ."

That is the attitude that the elder brother possessed. I want to show you three things that sadly show the spiritual slide of this man.

As we look at him, let's look at ourselves and decide if we are the prodigal who left home or the one who stayed home.

I. THE STAY-AT-HOME PRODIGAL WAS UNCONCERNED

"[The] *elder son was in the field.*"—Vs. 25.

The elder son came out of the fields after putting in a full day of strenuous chores. His day started at dawn and concluded at dusk—he had milked the cows, fed the chickens and plowed the fields. But there is not one indication in this account that the elder son ever lifted a finger to locate his lost brother. The Bible states that he came in from the *field*, signifying that the most important things in his life were raising the crops and harvesting them. But he showed little or no interest in his brother's whereabouts or in the fact that he was away from home and away from his father. He was untroubled, uninterested, unmoved and unconcerned about his younger brother.

We are prodigals at home when we are unconcerned.

"Awake to righteousness, and sin not; for some have not the knowledge of God: I speak this to your shame."—I Cor. 15:34.

It is to the believers' shame that they have unsaved family members for whom they've never prayed at the altar even though they share the same last name.

Sometimes when I'm preaching a revival meeting, by the third service I want to draw a map from the pew to the altar and hand it out to the people as they come into the service. Seemingly they have no clue as to where the altar is.

The altar is not made for bad people; it is made for people who have had God speak to their heart. You can outgrow your clothes, but you can never outgrow using an altar. Some folks haven't been to the altar since Theodore Roosevelt was president. It is to our guilt and our shame that we have not prayed at the altar for our family. It is to our embarrassment that we've never asked a soul winner to visit some of our lost relatives. It is to our remorse that we have unconverted family members to whom we've never presented the Gospel even though they share the same house address.

If believers became burdened for their lost family members and began to evangelize them, it would be a big enough task to keep each one busy for the rest of his life.

I think of my precious, godly mother, one of the greatest Christians I know. If you have a godly mother, you shouldn't give her a second's sorrow, and you shouldn't wait until Mother's Day to hug her neck. You need to appreciate her 365 days a year.

She recently told me that she went from cover to cover of her address book, and for every unsaved family member in our immediate family she got a one-year's subscription to the SWORD OF THE LORD. She didn't tell any of them what she was doing. I've got D. L. Moody and Charles H. Spurgeon preaching to my unsaved family members. Dr. John R. Rice and Dr. Tom Malone are making soul-winning calls through its pages.

Word is trickling back to my mother: "Someone has been sending us a paper, and we're enjoying it."

That is having a burden, a concern and a broken heart for those in her family who are not saved.

In a little cemetery beside an English church in India are buried people who were victims of a mutiny. There are no gravestones. No names are mentioned, no dates of birth or death are given, and no next of kin are named—only a single monument with one heart-wrenching word inscribed on it: "Forsaken."

We could erect monuments all over the world with that one word on it because of the prodigals who have stayed home and have forsaken their loved ones.

II. THE STAY-AT-HOME PRODIGAL WAS UNHAPPY

"He was angry, and would not go in."—Vs. 28.

The elder son was angry when he learned from the servants that his younger brother had returned and that their father had received him and that everyone at the house was rejoicing.

Instead of being *glad* that his brother had come home, he was *galled;* instead of being *merry,* he was *mortified;* instead of being *happy,* he was *unhappy.*

This is the same wrong spirit that is displayed when your church has a big day breaking old attendance records, scores of people are born again, and you gripe and grumble about a bus kid running through the fellowship hall!

The same spirit is demonstrated when your church has a great meeting—the preaching is hot, the music is scriptural, and the attendance is high—but you gripe and grumble because the air-conditioning made you too cool.

When God is blessing and all you can do is grumble and complain about the minuses—you are unhappy, miserable and uncomfortable—you are a prodigal at home and just as backslidden as can be!

I am weary of Christians who are never joyful, never excited, never happy about anything. A Christian ought to find something good in every bad situation.

O God, deliver us from bellyaching Christians!

We need to be on our spiritual guard at all times, because the Devil will throw a stick in the spokes of everything in which we are involved. He will try at every turn to sidetrack us from what God wants us to do.

So what if it's a bit cool or a little hot in church or the bus kids made noise or somebody sat in your seat, take it in stride and get excited about being in church!

The Devil is in the details, and not everything will run smoothly or go just as you plan it. When you hit a speed bump or a pothole in the road, just say hallelujah anyhow. Don't let the Devil bring about disorder or division; see it through with a sweet spirit and a happy smile! That's what makes for precious memories and exciting times. It's always sweeter on the other side of moaning and groaning.

Do not be a prodigal at home who is always unhappy.

There are several serious things that will keep the Christian from being cheerful.

1. We lose our cheer by not reading God's Word. "I rejoice at thy word, as one that findeth great spoil" (Ps. 119:162).

Show me a believer who is always in a bad humor, and I'll show you a believer who has not been in the Holy Bible.

When a preacher tells me that he has a grump in his church, I tell him, "The next time he comes to you whining and moaning and wailing about something, don't even address that; instead, ask him if he's moving his Bible marker more than one page."

2. We lose our cheer by not reaching God's will. "That ye may prove what is that good, and acceptable, and perfect, will of God" (Rom. 12:2).

There is no such thing as being *up* in your spirit if you are *out* of the will of God. If you are unhappy, it's an indicator that you're not reaching God's will.

I decided a long, long time ago that I am not going to endure my Christian life; I am going to enjoy my Christian life. I am going to enjoy my Christian life whether or not you are enjoying yours.

Often when I call home while at a meeting, my wife will ask, "How was the service tonight?" I am always quick to tell her that I'm having a good time.

3. We lose our cheer by not regarding God's work. "He that goeth forth and weepeth, bearing precious seed, shall doubtless come again with rejoicing, bringing his sheaves with him" (Ps. 126:6).

The believer who willfully turns his back on personal evangelism also turns his heart from personal excitement. Soul winners are excited Christians.

One of the men from this church sat down with me after the service last night and told me about a Bible conference he had recently attended. He had won some people to the Lord at the airport, and he was still rejoicing about it.

If people mean business with God, God will mean business with them. When God uses a Christian to introduce someone to the Lord Jesus Christ, it will make that Christian happy.

I get weary of people who doubt the genuineness of other folks' converts when they haven't won anyone to the Lord themselves. They don't want to catch a fish; what they want is for the fish to hook himself, jump into the boat, fillet himself and then jump into the frying pan and cook himself.

O Christian, you need to realize that not reading God's Word, not reaching God's will and not regarding God's work will cause you to be an unhappy Christian.

Dr. George W. Truett, a great preacher of yesteryear, often used to tell the charming story of a little girl who was eating breakfast. She saw a ray of sunlight coming through the window, and it focused on her spoon. She put the spoon into her mouth and exclaimed, "Look, Mommy; I swallowed a spoonful of sunshine!"

Why not trade that shovelful of gloom and despair that you have for breakfast for a spoonful of sunshine!

The elder son was unhappy.

III. THE STAY-AT-HOME PRODIGAL WAS UNFORGIVING

"And he answering said to his father, Lo, these many years do I serve thee, neither transgressed I at any time thy commandment: and yet thou never gavest me a kid, that I might make merry with my friends:

"But as soon as this thy son was come, which hath devoured thy living with harlots, thou hast killed for him the fatted calf."—Luke 15:29,30.

The stay-at-home prodigal was unforgiving. He reminds his father of the span of time during which he has served him, how he never sinned against him and how he doesn't have a single thing to show for it.

When we take a spiritual spade to the plot of this son's words, we see the root of his wickedness: unforgiveness.

We can be a prodigal at home when we are unforgiving.

Ephesians 4:32 says, "Be ye kind one to another, tenderhearted, forgiving one another, even as God for Christ's sake hath forgiven you."

154

It is just as easy to be a prodigal at home as it is to be a prodigal out in the field. If you have unforgiveness or bitterness in your heart, you are just as backslidden as if you were sitting on a bar stool. This is not just my opinion; that's what the Bible says.

I would be rich if I had a penny for every time I've heard someone say, "Dr. Hamblin, you just don't understand how hurt I am because of what she said to me," or, "I have been mistreated." You know what your problem is? You're waiting for one of these talk show hosts to call so you can pour out your complaints to the world! That's not the answer—the answer is to build a bridge and get over it!

I know of folks who are still griping and complaining about not getting a handshake a decade ago!

In one church where I preached, I saw two couples always sitting together on the same pew. I thought, *What a blessing these couples must be to each another.* Later, one of the husbands came up to me and began to weep. He said, "I sit in church with my best friend and his wife. He led me to Christ, but our wives became angry with each other years and years ago, and they haven't spoken to each other since."

I said, "They never speak to each other?"

He said, "Never, not even hello or good-bye."

We want revival, but we're at odds with one another. We want God to bless, but we're at odds with one another. We might even want to go into a new building program so we can have a greater ministry and reach more people for God, but we sit at odds with other members of our church. This holds back the power, the blessings and the touch of Almighty God.

155

One day I received a phone call from a preacher with whom I hold a revival every year. He said, "I heard the other day that you have become the pastor of a fundamental church in Flint, Michigan. I've got you scheduled for a revival this year, and I need to know if you're going to be a pastor and also hold meetings or if you are just going to be a pastor?"

I said, "I'm not looking at a church, and a church is not looking at me. My resume is not floating around, no one is voting on me, and no one has voted on me. Whatever you've heard, it is not true. I'm taking my twenty-third lap in evangelism, and I believe I'm right where God wants me to be."

He was very upset and said he was going to call the guy who told him all these lies. I told him to forget it, and I didn't give it another thought.

The next day another preacher from New England called me and said, "I have heard from someone that you've taken a church in Taylor, Michigan and that this Sunday is your first Sunday. I just want to plead with you to reconsider and not leave evangelism."

I said, "Wait a minute. I am not looking for a church, and a church is not looking for me. My resume is not floating around anywhere. Nobody is voting on me. I am right where God wants me to be."

He said, "I heard it from my brother-in-law, who is a preacher. He said he got a letter from you on your letterhead saying that you'd taken a church in Taylor and you were canceling all of your meetings, and you had signed the letter."

I said, "You compare the signature on that letter with my signature where I signed your Bible, and you'll see that they don't match."

I believe that's called mail fraud. Can you believe that somebody would get my stationery, put a lie on it and sign my name to it?

If I could find the person who did that, I would forgive him. Why? Because if I have unforgiveness in my heart, I am the loser, not the person who tried to hurt me.

I said to my wife, "I've got so much to do! Besides getting ready for revival, I've got to make sure that my pulpit in Flint is covered and my pulpit in Taylor is covered; I've got to make reservations for two guest speakers and cut two love-offering checks. Oh, I'm so busy!"

The stay-at-home prodigal was unforgiving.

While holding a ten-day revival meeting in 1999 in Detroit, I had an unforgettable experience. I preached one night about believers forgiving other believers and unbelievers, and when I gave the invitation, the altar was filled with people doing business with God.

The pastor called on one of his best men to close in prayer—he not only drove a Sunday school bus, but he was also the bus mechanic who kept a fleet of five buses running. He was the preacher's right-hand man.

The man prayed something like this: "Heavenly Father, I thank You for speaking to my heart tonight. You know that for over thirty years I have had bitterness in my heart toward that physician who gave the wrong medication to my father and brought about his death. Lord, tonight I forgive him because You have forgiven me. I am getting right with You tonight."

That night he got right with God by forgiving as he was forgiven.

We've seen from the pages of the Bible that it is possible to be in the father's house—not out in the field or in the far country—and still be a prodigal.

Don't be like the unconcerned, unhappy and unforgiving prodigal who stayed at home. Get right with God tonight!

Chapter 15

IT HAPPENED AT MIDNIGHT

"Moses said, Thus saith the LORD, About midnight will I go out into the midst of Egypt."—Exod. 11:4.

Inside the pages of the Word of God there are many heart-moving events, some past and others future, that take place in the middle of the night. The midnight hour has always seemed to have a special significance, both to God and to man. Either consternation or courage comes to a person's soul when he hears the clock strike twelve.

In the Book of Exodus, there are ten great plagues that took place in Egypt: (1) the blood, chapter 7; (2) the frogs, chapter 8; (3) the lice, chapter 8; (4) the flies, chapter 8; (5) the murrain, chapter 9; (6) the boils, chapter 9; (7) the hail, chapter 9; (8) the locusts, chapter 10; (9) the darkness, chapter 10; and (10) the death of the firstborn, chapter 11.

The well-known Bible expositor G. Campbell Morgan once wrote: "He [God] had waited patiently for the effect of the plagues, allowing time for Pharaoh to relent and repent, all without producing any other effect than determined and willful and insolent opposition."

In Exodus 11:4, the prophet Moses tells us by the inspiration of the Holy Spirit that the tenth plague—the death of the firstborn—will take place at midnight. This is the first of fourteen times that the word "midnight" is used in the Bible.

159

In the Hebrew language, *midnight* means "in the middle of the night."

When God's clock strikes twelve midnight, it is time to pay attention. I want to focus on three such midnight events. They are heart-stirring experiences for those who hear them and heed them.

I. RETRIBUTION CAME "AT MIDNIGHT"

Retribution is another word for punishment or judgment.

"And it came to pass, that at midnight the LORD smote all the firstborn in the land of Egypt, from the firstborn of Pharaoh that sat on his throne unto the firstborn of the captive that was in the dungeon; and all the firstborn of cattle."—Exod. 12:29.

The prophet Moses tells us that because Pharaoh refused to release the children of Israel from bondage, the tenth plague—the death of the firstborn—swiftly swept across the entire country. So extended was its powerful reach that the Bible describes its aftermath this way: "There was a great cry in Egypt; for there was not a house where there was not one dead" (vs. 30).

It may seem elementary, but all of us should always remember how retribution came to a country simply because of its refusal to do what was right.

A burglar entered a USO center in St. Paul, Minnesota; his theft netted him $23.50. Before leaving the scene, he wrote a note to an employee that read, "I'm sorry I did this. There is coming a day when I'm going to pay." There is a payday for sin.

Here is Pharaoh, his family and the entire population of Egypt coming to that moment of payment for the slavery they forced upon God's people, their skepticism of God's man and their stubbornness toward God's Word.

Friend, you and I need to understand that retribution came at midnight! Proverbs 29:1 says, "He, that being often reproved hardeneth his neck, shall suddenly be destroyed, and that without remedy."

How can we Christians keep from crying and praying for America when we think about how we have been antagonistic toward righteousness while at the same time throwing our arms of acceptance around perverts, purveyors of pornography and pilferers of purity! We are ripe for the retribution of God. Let me give you a small illustration of how our country is going to Hell in a handbasket.

I was sitting in the Nashville airport waiting for a flight, and across the aisle sat a distinguished-looking, somewhat elderly couple. The lady was reading a local newspaper, and the man was reading a pornographic magazine. There was a time, and not too long ago, that no one dared read that kind of stuff in public. But here sat this couple—he was reading the pornography like an ordinary magazine, and she was unconcerned that he was reading it!

God help any nation that murders babies in its hospitals and doctors' offices, that sells liquor in its gas stations and passes out contraceptives in the schoolhouse.

God judged Egypt, and He *will* judge America! God judged Egyptians, and He *will* judge Americans! Retribution will come "at midnight." That's one reason Christians should attend church on Sunday morning, Sunday night and Wednesday night. If we don't have revival, we are headed for ruin and retribution.

In A.D. 79, Mount Vesuvius erupted for the first time. Pliny the Younger, an eyewitness to the eruption, described it in two letters to the historian Tacitus. Pompeii, an ancient port city of South Italy, was situated at the foot of the mountain. An earthquake in A.D. 63 did much damage to that city, but the eruption of Vesuvius completely buried it. It was not only a flourishing and prospering city, it was also a resort with many, many villas. The volcanic cinders and ash and lava have so preserved the magnificent ruins, that to this day you can see the brilliant colors of the wall paintings.

But with every turn of the archaeologists' spades, the debauchery and depravity of that Roman seaport are unearthed. Cities like Pompeii and nations like Egypt lasted just long enough to learn the heartrending lesson that God's sharp sword of judgment will eventually fall on every sinful society! God's midnight does come, and with it comes retribution.

II. RAPTURE WILL COME "AT MIDNIGHT"

"And at midnight [not noonday] *there was a cry made, Behold, the bridegroom cometh; go ye out to meet him."*—Matt. 25:6.

The Lord Jesus Christ taught in the parable of the ten virgins that His return will come when the spiritual clock strikes twelve midnight.

I am certain this is a spiritual timepiece and not a literal timepiece because of the way the Lord concludes that parable: "Watch therefore, for ye know neither the day nor the hour wherein the Son of man cometh" (vs. 13).

Several years ago when I was holding a revival meeting in a western state, I was having breakfast with a Christian man. He asked me, "Has the Lord given you any insight

162

and information on the rapture?"

I knew he was looking for a day and an hour; I dare say he was even looking for a circus. I said, "Oh, yes." (I really had his attention now!)

He looked at me over his burned bacon and soggy eggs and said, "What has the Lord told you?"

"The Lord told me that if He doesn't come today, He may come tomorrow; and if not tomorrow, then He may come the next day."

No man knows the day or the hour when the Lord will return, but it will happen when God's spiritual clock strikes twelve midnight.

Now, I know that the word *rapture* is not used in the Bible, but neither is the word *Trinity*—that doesn't change the fact that they both exist. There is a Trinity, and there *will* be a rapture.

There are several reasons why I know there will be a snatching away—a rapture—of the saints at midnight.

1. I know because the Scriptures say so. "Then we which are alive and remain shall be caught up together with them in the clouds, to meet the Lord in the air" (I Thess. 4:17).

Christians can be confident concerning the second coming, because the teaching of it is contained between the covers of this Book.

2. I know because the Saviour said so. "And if I go and prepare a place for you, I will come again, and receive you unto myself; that where I am, there ye may be also" (John 14:3).

The Saviour, who is the very personification of truth

(vs. 6), has promised to pull His people off this planet.

3. I know because the situation says so. "And as he sat upon the mount of Olives, the disciples came unto him privately, saying, Tell us, when shall these things be? and what shall be the sign of thy coming, and of the end of the world?" (Matt. 24:3).

If indications of the revelation, Christ's appearing for His kingdom, are all around us, then the event of the rapture must be pressing closer and closer upon us. There are no signs for the rapture, but conditions seem right for the revelation, and you can't have the revelation unless you first have the rapture.

There will be a snatching away because the Scriptures say so, the Saviour said so and the signs say so.

During a visit to a great automobile factory in Detroit, Dr. Donald Grey Barnhouse was fascinated by seeing loads of scrap iron shuttled onto tracks over which an electromagnetic crane was operating on elevated rails. The crane operator brought the magnet over the cartload of scrap and, with the flip of a switch, turned on the power. Instantly the contents of that cart, with the exception of two small pieces, flew into the air and became attached to the magnet. The crane then transported the scrap iron to the furnace, and when the operator turned off the power, the material dropped into the melting pot.

The two pieces that had not been attracted by the magnet were a broomstick and a piece of copper tubing—neither of which was made of iron or steel.

Aren't you glad, Christian, that there is coming a magnificent moment when a supernatural Magnet—the Lord

Jesus Christ—is going to pass over this world and all those who have been blood washed and born again are going to break Earth's gravitational pull; up and out they're going to go!

Oh, it's God's midnight again—the rapture at midnight!

III. REJOICING CAME "AT MIDNIGHT"

"And at midnight Paul and Silas prayed, and sang praises unto God: and the prisoners heard them."—Acts 16:25.

After the apostle Paul had made a demon come out of a damsel, he and his co-worker Silas were beaten, brought to the inner prison and bound in heavy chains. Their attitude in such a frightening circumstance is just as amazing to people today as it was to those prisoners centuries ago, for the Bible says, "Paul and Silas prayed, and sang praises unto God."

If most Christians today were in the same situation that Paul and Silas were in, they would be shouting and sulking, moping and pouting about their circumstances. Understand that rejoicing will come "at midnight" if we are like Paul and Silas, with our entire being centered on Jesus.

During a revival meeting I was preaching in Wisconsin, the pastor asked me to go with him to call on an inmate. As we entered, the guards searched us, we went through a metal detector, and then when we stepped behind the bars, we heard that blood-chilling sound of the lock dropping into place. On our way to this man's cell, we passed a game room (in addition to the board games, pool tables and table tennis tables, there were four different video games playing); then we passed the television lounge with its big-screen television; then we went by the weight room and the Olympic-sized swimming pool. I thought, *They've got it better here inside than I've got it at the motel where I'm staying this week.*

But it was much different in the jails in Bible times; those dreary, dirty, rat-infested dungeons were miserable places. Paul and Silas were bruised, broken, bleeding and bound— but hallelujah, not blue!

Paul said, "Silas, how about if we sing all three verses of 'Victory in Jesus'"? And sing they did! They sang and sang until midnight was approaching. They sang (I believe) every verse of every song they knew.

Then Silas said, "Let's sing 'Jesus Paid It All.'" (It's amazing that Silas and I have the same favorite hymn.)

Then Paul said, "Let's sing the Baptist Anthem: 'Amazing Grace.'"

They didn't pout or sulk or just put up with it—they rejoiced at midnight in the prison.

The Bible says, "Yet the LORD will command his lovingkindness in the daytime, and in the night his song shall be with me, and my prayer unto the God of my life."—Ps. 42:8. Day and night it should be so!

We must not forget that Heaven and earth have every right to expect a melody from the believer who finds himself in a midnight episode. If we can sing and have a song only when things are going well, then there's little difference between us and the lost.

Several years ago there came to the Midwestern Baptist College in Pontiac, Michigan a young girl by the name of Helena. She was diagnosed with a brain tumor, and the doctors had to do emergency brain surgery. The paralysis left her with a frozen facial expression. She is stooped of shoulder and slow of step, and she uses a walker to get around. But she kept coming to class. Her sister or mother came with her to carry her book bag. They sat through each class with her and took notes for her.

Whenever I saw her I'd say, "Helena, how are you this morning?" With her face frozen in that one expression, she would say with a slur, "I'm great, Dr. Hamblin. How are you?"

Now, friend, what was it that you were complaining about this morning? What was it that put you out and rubbed you the wrong way? What was it that caused that famous black cloud to follow you everywhere and rain on everybody's parade?

If you think about it for half a second, you can say, "I've got it made it in the shade, drinking lemonade."

I think it would be an interesting study to take pen and paper with us and write down people's favorite expressions.

Some say, "I'm so tired." They say it today, they'll say it tomorrow, and they'll say it next year.

Some say, "I'm in a bad mood." They are always in a bad mood; they're even in a bad mood when they're in a good mood because they're not in their comfort zone of being in a bad mood.

How about this one? "I don't feel good." It doesn't matter what the question is—How was the revival? How was the conference you attended last month? How was your last meeting?—they always answer, "I don't feel good." Talk to them about nuclear physics, and they will answer the same.

An expression that was often used by a well-known preacher who has now been with the Lord for many, many years was, "Happy on the way." Whenever he was spoken to or asked a question, he would answer, "Happy on the way."

One afternoon a member of his church saw him in a

funeral procession; he was in the second car right behind the hearse, which was carrying the earthly remains of his loved one. There was no air-conditioning in automobiles at that time, so the windows of his car were rolled down.

Thinking he would get a different response on such an occasion, the church member called out, "Preacher, how are you today?"

With a song in his heart and a tear in his eye, he said, "Happy on the way." His rejoicing came "at midnight."

Many of you readers probably have broken hearts and exhausting burdens. Just recently I was with someone facing pain, and it would have been so easy for him to have thrown up his hands and have said, "I give up!" But there was a song in his heart, because he was rejoicing "at midnight."

We've seen from the pages of the Bible the prominence of the word *midnight*. It is an important hour to God, and it ought to stand out in its significance for those who are saved and those who are unsaved. How can it be important to the unsaved? Because it is a serious and strong reminder that good times are going to end, bad times are going to come and judgment is right around the corner for the one who hardens his heart and tramples underfoot the blood of Christ, doing despite to the Spirit of grace.

What will you feel at the midnight toll—fear or faith, courage or consternation?

Retribution came, and it will come again at midnight; the rapture will come when God's spiritual clock strikes twelve midnight; rejoicing can come at midnight. But until the final rejoicing at midnight, are you "happy on the way"?

Chapter 16

BURN, BROTHER, BURN!

Some of our churches have become spiritual refrigerators, and their members are little more than spiritual Popsicles. This would soon change with the coming of the heartwarming, supernatural combustion of the burning bush, and the members would soon become blazing believers. Somewhere we need to get hold of that which will cause us to "Burn, Brother, Burn!"

"Now Moses kept the flock of Jethro his father in law, the priest of Midian: and he led the flock to the backside of the desert, and came to the mountain of God, even to Horeb.

"And the angel of the LORD appeared unto him in a flame of fire out of the midst of a bush: and he looked, and, behold, the bush burned with fire, and the bush was not consumed.

"And Moses said, I will now turn aside, and see this great sight, why the bush is not burnt.

"And when the LORD saw that he turned aside to see, God called unto him out of the midst of the bush, and said, Moses, Moses. And he said, Here am I.

"And he said, Draw not nigh hither: put off thy shoes from off thy feet, for the place whereon thou standest is holy ground.

"Moreover he said, I am the God of thy father, the God of Abraham, the God of Isaac, and the God of Jacob. And Moses hid

his face; for he was afraid to look upon God."—Exod. 3:1–6.

The primary interpretation of this passage is that it describes the nation of Israel, which, although God dwelt in her, suffered from the persecutions of the many enemies who were not consumed or destroyed.

The practical interpretation is that it describes the believer who draws close to God and whose life is spiritually set ablaze because of it. I call that an individual revival, and every believer desperately needs such a burning-bush experience.

There is a crowd that likes to use the word *experience*. In the past we have surrendered some good words to that crowd, but this word is one that every believer should hold on to, and it is still a proper word for us to use.

I had an experience this very morning in the service. God met with us; He spoke to hearts and moved among us—that is an experience. I had an experience this afternoon that I consider a privilege. I was out soul winning, trying to win people to Christ. I am having an experience now as I stand here in this pulpit.

I refuse to have an experience with the Lord and not proclaim it to the world.

The burning-bush experience affords us some special things.

I. WHEN THE BUSH BURNS, IT WILL BE PERSONAL

"The angel of the LORD"—the incarnate Christ—stood before Moses and shared with him what was to be his sacred path. The deliverance of God's people from Pharaoh's hand and Egypt's land was a personal assignment given to Moses.

Don't miss this golden nugget from this verse: Before

God gives the believer a supernatural duty, there is always first a special dialogue.

"And the angel of the LORD appeared unto him in a flame of fire out of the midst of a bush: and he looked, and, behold, the bush burned with fire, and the bush was not consumed."

"Come now therefore, and I will send thee unto Pharaoh, that thou mayest bring forth my people the children of Israel out of Egypt."—Exod. 3:2, 10.

Too many believers who have not first had that special dialogue want that supernatural duty. You cannot have a verse-10 experience (the duty) without first having a verse-2 dialogue.

The greatest difficulty an evangelist deals with during a revival meeting is the church's desire to experience sinners getting saved, auditoriums being packed and saints becoming excited, while not one single church member expects a spiritual awakening for himself.

The Bible teaches that a revival never starts with the multitudes; it always starts with a man. The middle letter of the words revival, pride and sin is "I"; we'll never have revival until the *I*s have individual revival. There'll not be a revival in a collective way until we have revival in a personal way. It starts with "I" as an individual.

Gipsy Smith, a great evangelist, was asked, "How does one go about having a revival?"

He said, "Go home. Lock yourself in your room. Kneel down in the middle of the floor and draw a chalk circle around yourself. There, on your knees, ask God to send revival within that chalk circle. When God answers your prayer, the revival will be on."

171

Find a place at the altar, draw a spiritual chalk circle around yourself and ask God to send revival within that circumference.

II. WHEN THE BUSH BURNS, IT WILL BE PURIFYING

"And he said, Draw not nigh hither: put off thy shoes from off thy feet, for the place whereon thou standest is holy ground."—Vs. 5.

Moses was told to pull the sandals from his feet because the ground upon which he was standing was "holy ground." That is pure soil. (By the way, this is the first time the word *holy* appears in the Bible.)

Someone said, "God had to correct Moses' manners. Although he had been brought up in Pharaoh's court, he didn't know enough to take off his shoes in the presence of a holy God."

When we meet with God and have a revival (not simply a meeting or a series of services), it will be a purifying experience every time.

You can see the filth of this world on billboards that border on the pornographic. We can seldom listen to the radio, turn on the television or read the newspaper without hearing and seeing the world's garbage. But, oh, when we have a burning-bush experience, it will cleanse us and clear out the things in our lives that are not holy; it is truly a purifying experience.

There are several things that will cleanse the Christian.

1. There is cleansing in the cross. "[Jesus Christ] gave himself for us, that he might redeem us from all iniquity, and purify unto himself a peculiar people, zealous of good works" (Titus 2:14).

If the Saviour could give His life for us on Mount Calvary, then there is nothing that we cannot give up for Him.

2. There is cleansing in the communion. "Draw nigh to God, and he will draw nigh to you. Cleanse your hands, ye sinners; and purify your hearts, ye double minded" (Jas. 4:8).

The closer a believer gets to God, the easier it is to get rid of those things in his life that get in the way of God. There is no toy, temptation or trinket that the Devil waves in front of a believer that should mean more than a sweet relationship with God. When you get close to God, you want to get closer still.

Thank God if you are saved, but you will not have an intimate fellowship with God if you have not gotten things out of your life that interrupt your fellowship with Him.

3. There is cleansing in the coming of Christ. "Every man that hath this hope [the coming rapture] in him purifieth himself, even as he is pure" (I John 3:3).

If you keep the doctrine of the rapture on your heart, you won't have any difficulty doing right, because you'll understand that Jesus could return at any moment and catch you red-handed as you purchase a lottery ticket, draw on a cigarette, read a pornographic magazine, listen to perverted music or watch a filthy video.

Oh, if every Christian would realize that the things that will cleanse and purify him are the cross, the communion and the coming of Christ.

A teenage girl was converted, and her heart was thereafter flooded with love for her Lord. She wanted to please Him in all that she did and be the best witness for Him that she could be, but she wasn't sure where to draw the line about certain kinds of worldly amusements.

She went to her pastor with this problem, and he said, "Christ is now your Companion. Will your going to questionable places strengthen your daily walk with Him? Can you invite Jesus to accompany you and take part in these things? Were Jesus to come when you are in a questionable place, would you be ashamed to be there?"

"Thank you," she said to her pastor. "When I'm in doubt about anything, I'll seek to please Jesus."

A Christian will not find it hard to know where to draw the line if he has a burning-bush experience, because it will be purifying.

III. WHEN THE BUSH BURNS, IT WILL BE POWERFUL

"Come now therefore, and I will send thee unto Pharaoh, that thou mayest bring forth my people the children of Israel out of Egypt."—Exod. 3:10.

God spoke to Moses and revealed to him that he would be the leader who would show God's people sweet deliverance. This task was not a scoutmaster leading a Boy Scout troop into the backyard for an overnight campout for a merit badge. We're talking about one man leading a nation from its bondage of many years to the place of God's promised provision for them. If anyone needed divine help, divine strength, divine power and a divine wherewithal, it was Moses!

Every Christian needs to have a burning-bush experience because it is powerful. "We have this treasure in earthen vessels, that the excellency of the power may be of God, and not of us" (II Cor. 4:7).

On Monday morning a lot of preachers are ready to throw in the towel and quit the ministry. Other preachers start the week by just glowing over Sunday's service—the attendance, the offering, the filled altars, the good fellowship. A preacher should rejoice at the beginning of a new week, not be depressed about it. Monday should be a delight, the beginning of week-long opportunities. That doesn't mean that a preacher doesn't feel the responsibilities of his office or the duties listed on a full calendar. But when his ministry is given over to the Lord, He will help him get everything done—often to the amazement of the preacher!

My schedule is such that I will end one meeting and sometimes have less than twenty-four hours before I start another meeting. Sometimes I feel physically weary, and I'll pray, *Lord, I'm a bit tired. I'm weary and I feel spent. If anything is going to happen tonight, You are going to have to do it!*

Then I step up to preach, and God gives me that extra boost of strength to do what He has called me to do; He blesses in a marvelous way. This can be attributed only to Him. And that night as I pillow my head, I say, "Isn't God good!"

A burning-bush experience is powerful, and we'll be amazed at the pace we keep, the tasks that we complete and the way God is pleased to use us.

It is impossible even to imagine what the Sunday school class, bus route, visitation and soul-winning programs, church service or revival meeting would be like after a burning-bush experience in the lives of the church members.

Sunday school teacher, if you want to have a great class,

then between now and next Sunday have a burning-bush experience. You may be meeting in the corner of some room of the church with only two members in your class, but if you have a burning-bush experience, God will bless you and use you. Those two will find out that He has given you what you need and what they need, and two will become four, four will become six, six will become eight, etc.

I've known church bus drivers who have walked closely with God and had burning-bush experiences. Their buses became billboards on wheels; people they hadn't even visited saw them driving around the town, read the church name on the side of the bus, then got in their cars and followed them to church.

A preacher needs a burning-bush experience, but what would happen if his entire staff had the same experience? What kind of services would a church have if people in key positions of the church had a burning-bush experience?

What about a burning-bush experience during revival? It would soar to the heavens, climb to a new plateau and fill up the history books of the church. What a meeting we would have!

Dwight L. Moody would sometimes point to a special experience that he had on Wall Street when God did something special to him.

> One day in New York, what a day! I can't describe it. I seldom refer to it; it is almost too sacred to name. I can only say that God revealed Himself to me. I had such an experience of love that I had to ask Him to stay it.

> I went to preaching again. The sermons were no different, I did not present any new truth, yet hundreds

were converted. I would not go back where I was before that blessed experience.

Mr. Moody's preaching was never the same after that experience.

Doesn't your heart hunger for a happening like that? Wouldn't you like to see God do something in your heart that you could point back to and say, "Oh, I seldom can refer to that experience; it is almost too sacred to name. God did something to me that changed my life forever"?

When one has a burning-bush experience, there is a marked difference in the life of that believer. When that fire of God lands in you, it is an experience unexplainable and unforgettable. How about it, dear friend? Is the fire of God burning in you?

Dr. John N. Hamblin has been in full-time evangelism since 1980. During that time he has held hundreds of meetings in fundamental churches all across America and Canada.

He teaches in the Bible department at the Midwestern Baptist College in Pontiac, Michigan. Besides serving on a number of other fundamental boards, he is also a cooperating board member of the Sword of the Lord.

Pastors who have had Dr. Hamblin in their pulpits have called him "a Bible preacher of note," "a powerful revivalist," and "a pastor's friend."

Dr, Hamblin has authored a gospel tract, *God Has a "Gift for You!"* which is being used by nearly one hundred fundamental churches throughout America and Canada and has been translated into four different languages for use on foreign mission fields.

For a complete list of books available from the Sword of the Lord, write to Sword of the Lord Publishers, P. O. Box 1099, Murfreesboro, Tennessee 37133.

(800) 251-4100
(615) 893-6700
FAX (615) 848-6943
www.swordofthelord.com